Crazy Money

Jason Moore, CFP®

Embracing the Oddities of Our Financial Mind

Dedication

To my incredible students over the years. Your fascination, engagement, excitement, and curiosity encouraged me to write this book.

To my amazing wife Sarah. I have no idea how or why you tolerate me, but I am incredibly grateful you do. I Love you always.

Part One: Introduction to Biases and Logic Fallacies

Part Two: Discovering Your Money Story

Part Three: Cognitive Biases in Personal Finance

Part Four: Emotional Biases in Personal Finance

Part Five: Overcoming Biases in Your Financial Planning

Part 1: Introduction

Chapter 1

Why This Book and Why Now?

"Money is only a tool. It will take you wherever you wish, but it will not replace you as the driver." - Ayn Rand

Ten years. This is how long I have been teaching finance at Wright State University in Ohio. Over the course of those ten years, I have taught thousands of students. While I have been assigned to many different courses, my favorite by a mile is Personal Financial Literacy. Known among the staff as simply 2050 (Twenty-Fifty), this class has become an incredibly popular elective for all majors. Most sections of the course have a long wait list, and I am sure we could add two or three more sections each semester and have no problem filling them. This course focuses entirely on teaching students all the ins and outs of handling their own finances. Over the course of fifteen weeks the students learn everything from budgeting to insurance to investing for the future. They learn how to purchase a house and how to look at mutual funds. It's a wide-ranging class that has obvious appeal. Who doesn't want to know how to better control their personal finances? In fact, I declare to my students every time I teach the course, "You will take 4 years of classes here at WSU to prepare for a job making good money. This is the only course you will ever have that shows you what to do with it." I am amazed at the success stories of former students. They graduate with drastically increased credit scores. Some are purchasing their first home only a couple years out of school. I receive emails all the time from former students expressing their excitement at some new financial milestone. This course is truly one of the rare classes that benefit the students for the rest of their lives and brings me a personal sense of joy for leaving the world just a little better. It all feels so perfectly stitched together.

Yet, despite the large number of successes there are also failures. Clearly not every student who has taken my class over the past decade has gone on to financial independence. For many years I struggled to understand why. What was the difference? Was there a dramatic difference in attendance? Not that I could tell. Was it desire and interest? While I certainly understand some people will be more excited about a topic, I can't imagine anyone is totally uninterested in their OWN financial well-being. The information provided is the same across the board. It can't be a knowledge gap. So why success for some and not for others? This question perplexed me for years. Then as it so often does, inspiration struck from an unexpected place.

I was sweating (and singing) my way through another workout at the local gym. This is a place I have been most mornings for a decade or longer. Every morning it's conversations with other locals and long-time workout junkies. In between one of my personal karaoke sessions (much to the chagrin of my buddies I'm sure) I struck up a conversation with a gentleman who always has incredibly interesting ideas. He is an avid reader and likes to experiment with different strategies for good health. He mentioned how he would like to drop a little weight and wanted to know what I thought the best eating options would be. We discussed the usual "more vegetables, less

7

bacon" type stuff. He said something to the effect of, "I know that's the best choice, but I just really don't want to do it". In hindsight this moment and its lesson seem so obvious I am ashamed it took me so long to recognize. This highly intelligent, well-read, rational human KNEW the answer. He just didn't care. There was something in his behavioral psychology that was ignoring facts and logic and going its own way. He referenced a comment I had made a couple years earlier. I like to tell people who are worried about their weight, "the weight on the scale doesn't matter, what matters is your *mirror* weight". It's how you FEEL about your weight that decides your happiness level. If a person is trying to convince themselves to eat better and workout more but doesn't mind the person in the mirror, then the plan will never work. Their brain will sabotage them. The weight as determined by a scale is factual, but not as powerful as your self-image. How you PERCEIVE your health and weight are what truly drives you to change or not. It doesn't change the scientific fact you would be healthier at a lower weight, but that doesn't matter at all if you can't convince yourself you need to change.

As I thought about this conversation later in the day it hit me over the head how this applied to my students. There was no knowledge gap. There was simply a lack of mental commitment. I don't mean this in a negative way. Something was happening in their brains (and the brains of all of us) which was overriding what they knew to be the best financial decisions. This was a psychology and behavior issue, not a knowledge issue. This insight led me to the world of behavioral finance. The psychology field as it relates to personal finance is still very new, and many kinds of research are underway to fully grasp how it impacts our financial decision making. In this new frontier, however, I discovered the missing piece I had been so desperate to find. This was why students who received the same information made such wildly different, and sometimes damaging, choices. Their money brain was acting crazy.

Armed with a new outlook on how to teach financial literacy, I began incorporating small doses of behavioral finance into my classes. I was still a novice myself, but I wanted to know if this way of thinking about money could help more students over the hurdle. I began with the easy topics and soon realized the students were completely engaged in the lessons. Just as I had experienced the aha moment, they were now making the same connection. The underlying reasons for some of their poor financial choices made a little more sense. The way stores were trying to sell them things made just a little more sense. The reason two people armed with the same knowledge could make such wildly different choices made a little more sense. Each semester I continued to add more and more pieces around the psychology of money. Each semester the students responded with more and more enthusiasm. A nerve cord had clearly been struck.

I knew was on to something, but I faced a problem. My own limitations. I was not an expert by any stretch of the imagination. Far from it. I was researching all I could and devouring any books available. I was committed but needed to find a way to consolidate my new passion into a plan. I decided on a second master's degree. I sought a program that would place a heavy focus on Behavioral Finance and Financial Therapy. The answer, Kansas State University. The university's programming and instructors are amazing and allowed me to develop more skills and experience in the realm of behavioral finance. My students will reap the benefits of this training, and now so will you, dear reader. While I certainly have more to learn and still would not dare call myself an expert, I do understand the topic well enough to guide you on a journey of exploration.

The other question posed by this chapter title is WHY NOW? The answer to this question is three-fold. First, a very easy technical answer. The CFP (Certified Financial Planner) Board has finally acknowledged the importance behavioral finance plays in a person's decision making and planning. For this reason, they have added lessons and knowledge in the topics to the national test for certification. This means any university wishing to have its graduates sit for the CFP exam (of which Wright State is one) must begin teaching components of what you will find in this book.

The second reason for writing this book now is more personal. I have told you my story of enlightenment when it comes to teaching financial literacy. I firmly and whole-heartedly believe understanding the way your mind thinks about money is the key to becoming financially successful. There can be no other explanation for why some people continue to fail. The knowledge gap with regards to personal finance is gone. Any person can quickly do an internet search and have the basics of any topic in finance explained to them. Credit scores have become demystified and available on a phone app. Insurance is explained on approximately 47 million different internet sites (rounding to the nearest 47 million). You can use your phone, tablet, or computer to access dozens of budgeting tools. Even the secret curtain on the stock market has been pulled back. There are literally dozens of apps a person can use to purchase fractional shares of a stock. Stock market participation is soaring as a result. These are all positive movements forward in closing the knowledge gap. So why aren't people getting wealthier? Why aren't savings rates climbing? Most importantly, why aren't people feeling more satisfied with their money? It all comes back to my belief in our financial minds. Until we understand what is happening in our brain and how we can control or change it, no amount of technical knowledge is going to help.

The final reason for choosing now as the time to compile a book like this is simply the lack of anything close to similar being available. During my research and study of the topic and my completion of graduate work, I read many books discussing behavioral finance. All of them were incredibly dry and too academic to be useful to an everyday reader wishing to better their own financial life. They contained too much technical jargon. They discussed the details of different techniques used in various studies of the topic. I completely support the need for such books as this field is still young, and much work is being done every year to expand the universe of our knowledge. However, I believe most readers want a book that explains what the heck is going on and how they make immediate changes to improve their life. If that is you, then you are in luck.

My hope for this book is to bring humor and levity to a serious topic. I want to show you the crazy ways you think when it comes to money. I want to provide stories and examples that you can picture happening in your own life. After we explore all these bonkers things our brain is doing to us, we get to discuss what to do about it. When you have finished your journey through this book you will have a better insight into the flawed, but completely natural ways your brain is sabotaging your financial future. More importantly you will be equipped with the knowledge and tools to do something about it.

Chapter 2
What This Book is......and is NOT

As we begin this journey down the rabbit hole of your financial brain, it's important to set some clear guidelines about what to expect from this book. Let me start with a very simplistic overview. This book IS a humorous and light-hearted attempt to help you understand the strange and goofy ways your brain interacts with the financial world. This book is NOT a textbook. While all of this might seem straight forward, please allow me a moment of your time to elaborate.

I have spent the past few years learning all I can about this subject. I am truly fascinated by it. I have also presented it many times to both college students and corporate clients. I know the powerful impact this information can have on people. I have seen couples alter their retirement goals and watched the stress melt away as they realized most of their fears were inside their mind and not reality. I have helped companies drastically increase their 401(k)-participation rate by helping employees recognize why they were avoiding investing (see end of this chapter for a quick story). I have seen students develop better initial money habits by addressing their thought patterns right out of the gates and avoiding the early mistakes so many of us (me included) made. By writing this book I aim to shine a light on the dark spaces of your mind. We want to clean out that mental closet where all the bad financial thoughts have been hiding. Your mind is an amazing machine, and you can learn to control it. Well at least when it comes to your money thoughts. Your love life is all you.

Now for the details of what I specifically want to avoid in this book. Boring stuff. It's that simple. You came here (or you were forced here) to enjoy a quick funny read. I want you to think and laugh and come away with some tangible real life changes you can make immediately. I am not interested in overwhelming you with the mountains of research and data that back up the concepts. If research is something you are interested in there are dozens of heavy volumes you can investigate. The world of behavioral psychology is a deep pool with generations of studies to back it up. The world of financial psychology is new and constantly evolving. The truth is any research I quote to you might be out of date by the time this book even hits the shelves. More importantly, if you are the average reader, you don't care. I make a solemn vow to you everything I talk about in this book has been researched and studied. I am presenting it to you in a way that remains true to science and research while also being entertaining and enjoyable. After all, what's the point of writing a book meant to change people's lives for the better if they don't want to read it.

So here is the bargain I propose we strike up. I will do my very best to give you a fun read along with useful everyday tools, spread out over a couple hundred pages or less. I will also call you out on your special version of money crazy if I need to. You agree not to hold me to some ridiculously high research and citation standard like I am actually a smart person. You will treat me and this book like the idiot I am. You will also try your best to use the things you learn to better your life financially. If you agree to these terms, go ahead and turn the page. If you don't agree to these terms, turn the page anyways. You already bought the book and as your new (self-appointed) financial advisor I am telling you it would be wasteful to stop now.

*Bonus Story.

I promised I would swing back around and tell the story of how behavioral finance played out in a real time setting. I was asked to speak to a group of about one hundred employees at a local non-profit. This company does amazing work for the community but was struggling to encourage employees to take advantage of their retirement plan. At the time of my presentation there were only twelve people in the retirement program. So, I decided to try something different.

When I got up in front of the crowd, I asked two simple questions. "How many of you have heard someone from the company explain how important saving for retirement is?" Every hand went up. "How many of you believe it's important to save for retirement?" Again, every hand. This wasn't a knowledge issue. This was a psychological issue. So, I told them I was going to explain three psychological biases preventing them from committing to something they knew was in their own best interest. I spent about thirty minutes telling them why they weren't investing as opposed to telling them they should. We joked and laughed our way through examples (like you will see in this book) that highlighted how crazy they were acting. In the end, I watched almost thirty new people sign up. To be clear, there will need to be follow-up to make sure they stay on course. Financial psychology isn't a magic bullet, but it was pretty awesome to watch.

Chapter 3
Impact of Psychology on Financial Planning

As we begin to let the story unfold throughout this book, I believe it's important to take a step back and understand my philosophy on personal financial planning. This is relevant as it forms the connection between the technical side of finance and the behavioral side. If you understand how I approach financial planning, it will begin to make more sense as to why I am so passionate about people learning and mastering the psychological pieces of their financial life. Near the end of this book, I will provide what I believe are practical everyday strategies to improve your financial outlook. However, for now I want to keep us at a higher level and explain why I built my advice the way I have for clients and students.

Let's Get Mental

The first point I must highlight may seem very strange coming from a person with my background. I am heavily steeped in formal academic training in finance. I have multiple graduate degrees all focused on the formulas and

17

forecasting expected of someone in finance. I have been schooled (literally) on the best ways to predict market returns, project budgets, do risk analysis for insurance etc. Yet, I don't believe in any of it beyond a surface level. I know, that's crazy. Hear me out. I make this claim because I honestly believe money is not a technical discipline. It's a soft skill. This runs counter to everything I am supposed to stand for, but it lines up with everything I have experienced in working with real people. People DO NOT treat money as a technical science in their everyday lives. They just don't. We make financial decisions in the moment. We use a huge number of contextual factors, lifestyle preferences, and emotions. Finance is 99% MENTAL. This plays out in so many ways within our lives. Let me show you a few.

As you are likely aware, most of us struggle with decision fatigue. Our world is spinning so fast these days that many of us are experiencing a very real energy drain from the sheer number of decisions we must make each day. This decision fatigue causes two negative consequences. The first is poor decisions. As our mental energy falls, our decisions get worse. Duh. The second is decision avoidance. The best way to prevent a decision from eating up your energy reserves is to simply not make the decision. For this reason, I strongly encourage my clients to set up completely automated financial programs. Everything from investments to bill pay, to direct deposits. This keeps the client from using any energy at all for the decisions. Make it once and move on. However, all these things take a commitment. When it comes to setting up your 401(k) for example, the hard part is not picking the correct mutual funds. Just choose an index fund and move on. The hard part and what contributes 99% of the challenge is to COMMIT to setting aside 20% of your paycheck. That is NOT a financial analysis. That has NOTHING to do with picking the right stocks. It has everything to do with psychology. It's a behavioral choice. The reason automated investing (and all the other stuff) works so well is because I am not forcing my client to make the same difficult behavioral commitment over and over. From a purely technical perspective, it should not matter. Financial logic says you need to invest. So do it. Except, that's not how any of us view the world. We might KNOW it's the right thing to do, but that doesn't mean we will do it every time. It's psychology, not finance.

Next, I want to venture into the world of cars. We will explore this industry many times throughout this book. When it comes to choosing a vehicle, finance is very clear. Purchase the cheapest possible option to get you from point A to point B. Cars are a depreciating asset, which means we should avoid putting any significant amount of money towards them. But is that how you personally view your car? For a small percentage of the population, yes. For most people, a resounding no. Most Americans view their car as something else. It's a reflection of your personality. It's a sign of your career success. It's your escape from the stresses of the world. Whatever it may be, we have a passion for our cars. There is NOTHING financial about it. It goes against every rule of technical finance. Yet, we all do it. So as an advisor I have a choice. I can either stubbornly adhere to my training by insisting the client buys a cheap car and have my client tune me out completely, or I can acknowledge the reality of the world and help my client avoid a catastrophic mistake in purchasing a vehicle. My job is to help them understand what the car represents, what they are trying to accomplish with the car purchase, and what other sacrifices they might be willing to make to afford the car. Those are not financial questions (ok, the last one kind of is a little). They are psychological questions. They go to the heart of what the person feels and thinks.

I cannot stress this enough. The key to you becoming financially successful lies in your BEHAVIOR, not your technical financial knowledge. The awesome thing about that statement is it means ANYONE can do it. Your educational background, family upbringing, and income have nothing to do with it. Everyone can be better at finance simply by improving their behavioral patterns around money.

Time is Expensive

The second key point I want to bring up involves time. I always ask my students what the most important use of money is for them. I often get the basics like food, shelter, and other necessities. I don't really disagree with those answers, but I think they miss the mark. To me, the most important thing money can do is buy you time. I mean this in the most literal sense. You are using your money as currency to purchase time. When you get sick and need to be off work, having money in the bank provides you with time to heal. When you become stressed and need a break, money buys you time to take a vacation. If you stop and think about what retirement really is, it's having enough money to buy every minute of the rest of your life.

I explain this to all my clients in the most basic terms. Money buys you freedom. End of story. Every person truly desires to spend their time doing what they want, with the people they want, when they want, for as long as they want. Money provides that. It buys you the TIME to do those things. What that specific time looks like is different for everyone. This goes back to my earlier comments about finance being mental. I would ask you to stop and think about the following scenario deeply.

As your advisor, I just told you as of right now you can have all the time you will ever need to do what you want because you have enough money in the bank to retire. I ran the numbers and I am 100% positive based on our previous conversations about your dreams that you are ready. I make this claim because you have:

A. $500,000 in the bank

B. $1,000,000 in the bank

Or

C. $5,000,000 in the bank

My question to you is, "Do you actually care whether you have A, B, or C?" In the above scenario, what piece resonated most deeply with you? The dollar figures or the achievement? My guess based on doing this work for over

20 years is you responded most strongly to the part where I told you it's time. You are ready to go do what you want. The dollar figures NEVER represent anything more than numbers on a page. People don't think of life in dollar figures. We think of life in terms of experiences and emotions. So, say it with me again, that's psychological not financial.

You should begin to view your life's financial decisions through this prism. The account statements for all your savings and investments should be "translated" into the freedom and time they are buying you.

We Are All Babies

 My final commentary on how all this ties into your financial planning is to claim we are all novices. More accurately, we are all giant financial babies. You may not realize this, but pretty much everything about personal finance is an incredibly recent development. Quick rundown.

- Social Security - First payout made in 1937.

- Retirement - Did not even exist until the 1940's (and then only for a tiny percentage of people)

- 401(k) - Signed into law in 1978 (The very same year my amazingness entered the world. Obviously, I was destined to be in finance.)

- Roth IRA's - Came into being in 1997 (Seriously, this was AFTER I graduated high school. I want to cry.)

- Credit cards - First credit card was the Diners Card in 1950.

- New Car loans - 1919 was the first time we borrowed money for a new car.

- Credit Scores - Created in 1956, but the score you know of today (FICO) was introduced in 1989. You read that correctly.

- Student Loans - 1958. Ironically, most of us won't pay off our student loans until 2058.

- Crypto Currency - 2009 with Bitcoin. This ENTIRELY new form of money is only 14 years old.

I highlight all these dates to show you how much of your financial world has come into existence in the last 100 years or less. Compare to the amount of time humans have been running around stabbing each other on earth. The entire concept of personal finance, as we know it, is incredibly young. So, it should come as no surprise, we are still not very good at it. As a species we are trying to learn how to handle this whole thing. Take retirement for example. Should we expect to be awesome at the idea yet? The entire concept of not working until you die just became a real thing 80 years ago. The tools we use to fund our retirement were not a thing until the 1970's for goodness' sake. I mean, honestly, the ROTH IRA is barely old enough to vote and drink alcohol. Most people reading this believe credit scores are part of our DNA given to us at birth. Yet, there are millions of Americans alive who were born before they even existed.

I highlight these stories as a way of encouraging you. You may have made financial mistakes in your life. Most of us have. As humans, we simply haven't had the time to work out the kinks just yet when it comes to our financial life. The good news is you can get better. You can learn from mistakes you have made as well as others. The most important reason to consider the behavioral side of finance is because you and you alone control it. You will always and forever be in control of your own thoughts. If you can use this book to improve the way you THINK about money, you stand a good chance of improving your financial life. So, give yourself a mental break and set out to be better next time.

Chapter 4

Explanation of Cognitive and Emotional Biases

"Stop buying things you don't need, to impress people you don't even like." – Suze Orman

To begin this journey, it's important for me to lay a foundation as to what I mean by the concept of biases. Based on the current political climate there is a certain view of this word floating around. For the purposes of our time together it's important for you to realize I am NOT talking about biases as a shortcut for negative views of other people. While that is one form of bias, it is not being used in the same context for this book. Yes, it is technically true that biases formed around race and gender function in much the same way (after all it's a scientific term from psychology), but we are not going anywhere near that discussion. It has nothing at all to do with this topic. Instead let's craft a way of thinking about biases that we can both use for the remainder of our time together.

A good working definition we can use of a cognitive bias is a systematic pattern of deviation from rationality in judgment or decision-making. Cognitive biases represent mental shortcuts (heuristics) our brains use to process information and make sense of the world around us. The brain jumps through these mental hoops because evolution has taught our brain the importance of energy conservation. Using these mental shortcuts serves two purposes. First, it allows the brain to utilize far less energy as it can jump to a conclusion much faster and therefore turn off the power early. It is also a built-in survival method for our brain. When we humans lived in the jungles and any noise could mean a lion was about to make a meal of us, it was a good thing to react quickly. Even if that reaction was not fully rational. Better to overreact than be dead. In today's world we don't often face life and death situations, but the brain's hardwiring is still installed and hasn't had time to evolve into something better. So, the shortcuts remain embedded. However, these biases can lead to irrational or distorted conclusions, as they may not always align with objective reality or logical reasoning. Cognitive biases influence how we perceive, and interpret information, impacting our judgments, beliefs, and behaviors in various situations.

There is also a side of mental gymnastics that falls in the category of emotional biases. These biases highlight the influence of emotions on the way we perceive, interpret, and make decisions about information and events. Emotional biases impact our judgment and decision-making processes, leading us to prioritize certain emotions over rational decisions. These biases cause us to react or respond in ways that may not align with objective information or logical reasoning. Quick example. Did you know that new home builders love to bake fresh cookies in their model homes? Why? They do this because your brain associates baked goods with "home". So, it's a way to use an emotional connection your brain already has to bring about positive feelings while you are in the house. However, should the smell of the model home rationally be more important than the quality of the construction? Of course not. Emotional biases can manifest in various forms, such as making decisions based on fear, excitement, or a desire to avoid negative emotions. These biases can also influence how we remember past experiences or anticipate future outcomes, often leading to subjective and emotionally driven assessments.

Being aware of biases is essential for making more balanced and rational decisions, as it allows us to step back from our emotions and consider objective information when faced with important choices or evaluations. Understanding and managing biases can lead to better decision-making and more effective problem-solving. This specific idea of self-awareness and internal reflection is something we will return to in a later chapter as we explore how to counteract mental biases.

In this book I will be walking you through many different biases that play an outsized role in impacting our finances. I am dividing the list into cognitive and emotional biases. However, it's important to realize that many of them operate in the gray area between the two kinds. Our brain even makes being slightly crazy hard to pin down. I also want to fully acknowledge there are hundreds of possible biases. This book is FAR from an exhaustive list. What I am focusing on for your sake are the high impact items. These represent the biases most common in money issues and the most likely to be causing you financial hardship. My belief is after you delve into these and understand how they work and what havoc they are wreaking on your finances, you will naturally begin to pick out other biases in your thinking. It will become more second nature for you to recognize when your thinking is being influenced. Even if you can't name the new bias from the list of a million out there, you will know something strange is happening and take the appropriate caution.

So, my friend, that is what we are working with. This book is all about you understanding the mental shortcuts your brain is taking and why that's not always a good thing. When it comes to your money, you need a clear mind to make positive decisions. You can't let your brain lead you down the path of CRAZY MONEY. And away we go!

Part 2: Discovering Your Money Story

Chapter 5
Money Mindsets and Stories

Money Mindsets

 There is an interesting dynamic around decisions that comes directly from the world of traditional psychology. Every person believes the decision they are making is correct at the moment. That may sound like a strange statement but think of how it plays out in your own life. I have made many mistakes and bad decisions in my life, but for every one of them I believed it was the best decision in the moment. Even if I knew it was a "bad" choice or "wrong" according to society, I still had my own justifications for doing it. These internal rationalizations made it the right decision for me at that exact moment. Other people might disagree. Heck, after five minutes of self-reflection I might disagree. It doesn't change the fact at the very moment of the decision, I felt like it was the right choice.

I bring this concept up because it equally applies to our money decisions. When you judge yourself or someone else for what appears to be a crazy money choice, keep in mind it made sense to that person in the moment of decision. It is important to realize everyone comes to a decision about money from completely different circumstances. Where many financial advisors error is in believing all clients

30

should approach decisions the same way. After all, there are financial models for the technically correct answer to almost every financial choice. However, would you expect a child raised in extreme poverty with little to eat to approach grocery budgeting the same way as someone raised in the middle class? Should we expect a person who represents a minority population to have the same level of trust in the banking industry as a white individual when you recognize the history of prejudiced lending in our country? Should men and women view car buying in the same way when studies show dealerships charge women more for every new car purchase? (known as the Pink Tax) This list goes on and on. The fact will always remain that people come from every conceivable background and circumstance imaginable. For this reason, our view of money from a psychological perspective will always be different. This is why I stress you begin a process of self-evaluation around financial thoughts.

To begin the process of overcoming your money biases and developing a stable money psychology you need to know where you are right now. Let me give you two examples of what these mindsets can look like.

Poverty Mindset

When someone is raised in an environment of poverty, the very way they view finances is drastically altered. It can take years of therapy and internal work to break through these barriers. Here are a few challenges faced by someone stuck in the poverty mindset:

- People with poverty mindset view money as a finite resource, leading to a constant focus on scarcity. This results in heightened anxiety about finances and places a priority on short-term needs over long-term planning.

- People with a poverty mindset may have an aversion to spending money, even on essential items, due to the fear of depleting their limited resources. This can lead to difficulty making necessary purchases.

- People with poverty mindset create only survival-based financial goals, such as paying bills and meeting basic needs. There is no consideration of wealth-building, career advancement, or financial independence.

- People with poverty mindset avoid seeking financial education or advice, believing that financial literacy and wealth-building are unattainable or not relevant to their circumstances. They carry shame about their money situation.

You can see how this poverty mindset would be so destructive towards any future planning. People don't choose this mindset. Circumstances chose it for them.

Old Money vs. New Money Mindset

Another interesting way of looking at money mindsets involves families who have larger amounts of wealth. While we view all rich people as well rich, they aren't the same. It depends largely on the source of that wealth.

If you come from a family with a history of inherited wealth you may have the following OLD MONEY views:

- They believe money and wealth are completely normal, and everyone has it.

- They are normally conservative in their money approach because they are more concerned with preservation than growth.

- They may lack financial literacy because there is little need to learn about money when there has always been more than enough to go around.

- They often value heirlooms and other items that money can't buy because they CAN buy everything else.

We contrast this with NEW MONEY (self-made) views:

- They tend to be more aggressive because a high growth rate is how they achieved quick financial success.

- They tend to prefer flashier toys to show off their newfound wealth.

- They often understand various financial products because these tools were part of their plan to grow wealthy.

- They may struggle with Self-Control because their new wealth affords them things they were never able to purchase before.

You can see there is a huge difference in the psychology of these two groups, even if there is little difference in their bank accounts. We should not expect them to respond to decisions the same way.

Money Story

What does all this mean for you? Well, I want you to spend some time going through exercises of self-discovery. We are going to use a few question inventories to dig into your Money Story. A Money Story brings to life your experiences and background with money and allows us to understand how our current Money Mindset was formed. By understanding our Money Story, we can begin to undo some of the negative aspects of our current Money Mindset.

For example, if your Money Story involved being raised in a very wealthy family and getting anything you wanted when you wanted it, you might understand where your lack of Self-Control comes from. You might also realize you don't have any financial literacy because it wasn't required. In addition, it makes more sense why you struggle with Loss Aversion so badly. You are in preservation mode and afraid to take any chances. Now you have information about possible weaknesses in your Money Mindset that you can work on.

If, as you read through the bias chapters, you find yourself nodding along and thinking one of them really hits home with you, these exercises will hopefully shed some light on why. Like any psychological issue, recognizing it and accepting it are important first steps in changing it. We aren't going to attempt labeling your Money Mindset or

Money Story today. Instead, we will explore some of your thoughts around money and see where it leads us.

Instructions

After you answer each challenge think about these questions.

- Why did I respond that way?

- Was I able to answer quickly, or did I have to think about it?

- Did I answer the way I think society says I should, or the way I truly feel?

- Is there anything in my background influencing this answer?

- Do I honestly wish I could answer differently?

I highly recommend you write all this down, as a pattern will emerge. That is what you are looking for. It holds the key to why you handle money the way you do. Ready? OK, go.

Money Thoughts

I want you to take some time and think through the following philosophical challenges. Keep in mind there are no right or wrong answers. It's more important to place the answers in the context of your life.

- What is the most important use of money in a person's life? (*remember to answer the follow up questions before you move on.)

- Who do you think makes a larger impact on the world? Someone who spends their life in service to others or someone who builds a huge profitable corporation.

- If you had to choose between having all the money you could ever want or all the love you could ever want, which would it be?

- If you heard someone say, "Money doesn't matter" what would your initial reaction be?

- What if a different person said, "I love money". Now what is your reaction?

- How much money is enough?

- If you had to describe the type of person who is the "best" with money, what does he or she look like?

- How acceptable is it to talk about money? In public? Coworkers? Family? Friends?

Money Prompts

For this next exercise I want you to write down your initial thoughts to the following prompts. Think of this as a fill in the blank challenge. The key to this exercise is speed of response. If you really want to find the patterns in your Money Story, you must avoid answering the way you believe you are "supposed" to answer. Be true to yourself. If you don't like the answer, you can work to change that in your life. *Keep answering those follow up questions from the instructions.

- Most rich people got that way by___

- Adult children owe their parents___

- Financially I deserve to___

- Financially, I don't deserve to___

- A person should never spend money on___

- The relationship between money and love is___

- The worst thing someone can do with money is___

- Parents owe their children___

- Successful family members owe less successful family members___

- The best way to help my children (current or future) financially is___

Money Relationships

The third exercise I want you to work through is fleshing out your views on the way money interacts with other aspects of your life. Take a quick look at the table below and pick out whichever five or six words jump out to you. If you are a super overachiever, do them all. Once you have made your selections, write a short statement about how you view that word's relationship to money.

The rich	marriage
religion	politician
corruption	technology
death	status
dad	capitalism
the poor	fear
depression	anger
husbands	debt
sex	children
security	education
power	evil
food	wives
work	god
love	giving
savings	mom

Parent to Child training program

Next, you are going to develop a money training program for your child (Or future children. Or little kids you like. Just go with me here). I want you to think through the process of how you would teach a child about money. In doing so, answer the following questions?

1. What are the 5 main topics you want to focus on your child learning?

2. What message about money do you want your child to take away from the training?

3. Are there any misconceptions about money that you want to make sure are dispelled for your child during the program?

4. What tools (software, apps) would you like to see your child use?

5. How often will you introduce a new topic and how often will you review your child's progress?

6. How long do you think it will take for the child to develop solid financial habits?

7. Are there any areas of finance you are not worried about trying to teach your child?

8. What additional research or learning do YOU need to do before teaching it to your child?

Money History

The final exercise to think through might end up being a little painful. I apologize in advance for that. What I want you to do is delve into your personal background. We are seeking to uncover some of the pivotal points in your Money Story. What is the narrative of your upbringing as it relates to finances. So, take your time and think these through. This section is not about speed, but rather about depth.

1. What is the best money memory you have as a child? It could be a one-time thing (special birthday present) or a series of events (mom bought me a new book every time I got an A on my report card) However you define best is fine. It's your story.

2. What is the worst money memory you have and how do you feel it changed you?

3. Who was the controller of money in your life and how did that person treat money?

4. Do you remember ever being worried about money as a kid? Did this worry originate from your parents or another source?

5. Who taught you about money and how it works? (Before this book obviously)

6. Did you ever experience a singular moment in your past that forever altered your view of money either positively or negatively?

7. When was the first time you were exposed to the concepts of investments, insurance, budgets etc.?

8. Do you (now or in the future) hope to provide a similar money history to your children as the one you grew up with?

9. What is the most toxic behavior around money you can remember someone in your life doing as a child?

10. Do you hate me now for making you remember that one birthday where you didn't get the Easy Bake Oven you were dreaming of? Kidding. I hope this wasn't a painful walk down memory lane.

That's the ball game folks. My hope is you were able to discover some clear patterns in your history and then tie those to your current way of viewing money. These connections give us the insight to make the changes we desire. The realization there is a root cause to some of your problematic behaviors can assist you in overcoming them. Keep this in mind as we hop aboard the Crazy Train and barrel down the tracks into our brain's bonkers way of handling things.

Chapter 6
Money Disorders

 Now that you have taken some time to explore your own money background, I hope you will be more open to understanding how people develop challenges around their financial thinking. In this chapter I will introduce you to a few of the more destructive financial behavior patterns that can develop.

This conversation may feel heavier than much of this book. That is by design. While I always strive to have clients and readers view money in a positive light, the reality can be very different for some. I will introduce you to several financial disorders which can take over your life if you are not careful. However, fear not brave reader. In the next chapter I will explain to you the various therapy options developed by experts to assist in overcoming these challenges.

To kick us off I want to throw out a few scenarios so you can place yourself in someone else's shoes. (Though these scenarios may be your experience as well)

Client 1 – Stuck in Poverty Mindset

- Raised in a very poor household.
- Food and necessities were in short supply

- Forced to move multiple times
- Utilities being shut off was not uncommon
- Remembers parents getting calls from collection agencies
- Often embarrassed at school about their clothes or other items

If you were trying to assist this human being in creating a positive financial future, what challenges could you see in the planning process?

Client 2 - Divorced Female

- Husband handled all the finances during marriage
- Income was unequal
- Money was weaponized to control her
- Children will now be sharing time
- Many of her luxury items will now be unaffordable on a single income

What unique concerns might this client have? How could you reassure her the future will be better? Is that true?

Client 3 - Strict Religious Upbringing

- Family religion forced no holidays or birthdays
- Friends outside of the church were not allowed
- Education was frowned upon
- Money was seen as evil (or root of all evil as it were)
- Only males were allowed to hold authority positions
- Has since left the church

What difficulties might this client face in simply adjusting to normal life outside the church? Could you face challenges trying to convince this person to even care about money? What priorities do you believe this person might have when it comes to money?

Disorders Identified

I hope you begin to see many of the financial decision-making struggles people face are deep-seated issues resulting from prior experiences. Some of those past experiences are completely out of their control. To be clear, I am not excusing the huge number of people who have no such history of challenging circumstances. There are, to be sure, a multitude of individuals who are screwing up their financial future all on their own. However, I wanted to introduce some empathy to the conversation as well. Every person has a unique history and sometimes it continues to impact our present.

Now having laid the groundwork for a better understanding of how people find themselves battling negative financial behaviors, I'm going to introduce you to some very specific Money Disorders. Like other areas of mental health, we can group people into categories of disorder based on common behavior patterns. My ask of you is to read these and do a self-evaluation as you go. I hope you are not suffering from any of these currently, but we all must be mindful and vigilant moving forward. You should aim to identify which if any of these disorders you believe you might be susceptible to in the future. This acknowledgement and awareness can assist you in heading the problems off before they reach the level of full-blown disorder.

Compulsive Buying or Overspending (CBD)

We begin with the disorder most people will automatically jump to when thinking of money issues. It is not hard to imagine why this might be the case. Here in the U.S. we are obsessed with materialism. It's in our DNA. When you are the richest nation to ever inhabit the planet, there are going to be a lot of things to buy. There is also a drive to be part of the crowd. All these factors merge into a toxic cocktail influencing us towards overspending.

As you read the list of common traits, I want you to notice another important factor though. Emotions. This disorder is often associated with Retail Therapy. We shop and buy because we feel "down". We shop because we got a promotion at work. We shop because we are bored. We have allowed this to become our default solution to many of our normal daily emotions. It should be no shocker than this has become a huge issue and the most common disorder in finance.

Common Behavior Patterns:

- **Recurrent, Compulsive Shopping** - People with CBD experience an intense and uncontrollable urge to shop, often buying items they don't need or can't afford.

- **Emotional Triggers** - Compulsive buying can be triggered by negative emotions, such as loneliness, anxiety, or depression. Shopping provides a momentary "high", which only reinforces the behavior.

- **Feelings of Guilt or Regret** - After engaging in compulsive buying, we often feel guilt, shame, or regret over their spending. The cycle of guilt and buying creates a loop where we shop to relieve feelings of shame or anxiety.

- **Hiding Purchases** - People with CBD may attempt to conceal their shopping behavior from others.

- **Preoccupation with Shopping** - Those with CBD may spend excessive time thinking about shopping, planning their purchases, or seeking out new items to buy. You need to stop mindless scrolling on the shopping apps.

Workaholism

Well, I don't think I want to talk about this disorder. The reason being I suffer from it. As mentioned in the opening of this chapter, it's critically important we are honest with ourselves and identify potential areas of concern. This is mine. I feel an overwhelming sense of time slipping away. I want to make such a positive impact on the world and I have so many thoughts on how to do this. Sometimes I feel like the rabbit from Alice in Wonderful. "I'm late, I'm late for a very important date."

If you have this same issue, I give my strongest caution. I speak from experience you can allow even the positive momentum of a career to get away from you. Working all the time (even really good things) will eventually catch up with you. Please take some time to care for yourself during the process. If nothing else, consider it part of the working process. You can't continue to do all the positive things you are capable of if you break down.

As for the actual concerns contained within this disorder, I suspect you will not be surprised by any of them.

- **Compulsion to Work** – Persistent and constant preoccupation with work or to-do lists, even during personal or leisure time. (What is this leisure time they speak of?)

- **Excessive Hours** - Working significantly longer than required or reasonably expected.

- **Neglect of Other Aspects of Life** - Prioritizing work over family, social activities, and self-care. (This is the killer)

- **Stress and Burnout** - Often accompanied by chronic stress, anxiety, or exhaustion.

- **Anxiety When Not Working** - Feeling uncomfortable or restless during downtime. I cannot tell you how much I struggle with this. My wife always comments that I simply have no "Off" switch. Candidly, I get annoyed with myself sometimes when I can't wind down the engine.

Gambling

The next disorder on our list is such a tough nut to crack for a few reasons. First, there is at least a chance you actually come out ahead gambling. It's obviously going to be harder to break the habit when it actually works out for you. The reality that all gambling eventually leads to a downfall (they don't build casinos because YOU win) doesn't matter in the moment if things are currently going well. Second, gambling can be considered a social activity. Like drinking, this can be given a mask of social acceptability when done with friends. Lastly, gambling provides an adrenaline rush on par with illegal drugs such as cocaine. It very literally triggers the same pleasure sensors in the brain. This makes it really addicting in a way simply buying a pair of shoes can't match.

In the next section of the book, we will be covering some of the general therapy options available to help offset these disorders. However, for this specific disorder it is imperative you or your loved one seek professional counseling. It is next to impossible to overcome on your own.

- **Preoccupied with Gambling** - Constantly thinking about gambling, planning future gambling activities, or reliving past gambling experiences.

- **Increasing Tolerance** - Needing to gamble with increasing amounts of money to achieve the same level of excitement. Again, this is on par with drugs.

- **Suffer Withdrawal Symptoms** - Restlessness or irritability when attempting to reduce or stop gambling. See drugs!

- **Lying About Gambling** - Concealing the extent of gambling from family, friends, or therapists.

- **Jeopardizing Relationships** – Risking key relationships or jobs due to gambling.

- **Relying on Others for Money:** Seeking financial bailouts from others.

Hoarding

Well, this is awkward. I admitted above I have a workaholic issue. However, I have whatever is the opposite of this mess. If someone ever makes my life into a superhero movie, I would be cast as Anti-Hoarder Man. It would be a terrible movie, but it would be accurate.

On to the actual topic at hand. Hoarding is such a challenging issue to work through because it almost never has anything to do with your stuff. The "stuff" is just a fill in for the true underlying emotional damage. It can be any number of things (eg. Growing up poor, having overly controlling parents, traumatic loss of a loved one ....) and this makes it difficult for an outsider to pin down.

The positive side of the disorder is most individuals don't want to continue with it. They realize it's becoming an issue and more often than not are aware of the underlying trauma that led to it. Once a therapist begins working with them, the root cause can be identified in most cases without too much digging. If this is someone you know, you should seek help for them before the unrelated emotional damage causes permanent financial damage.

- **Difficulty Discarding Items** - Inability to part with possessions, even if they are broken, outdated, or of little value. Emotional distress or anxiety at the thought of discarding items.

- **Excessive Clutter** - Accumulation of items that congest living spaces.

- **Perceived Need to Save Items** - Strong attachment to possessions due to their perceived functional value. Fear of losing important information or opportunities tied to items. You can refer to a later chapter on the Endowment Effect to understand the impact of this.

- **Social Isolation** - Significant distress or impairment in social, occupational, or other important areas of functioning. Strained relationships and health risks.

Financial Denial (Avoidance)

This disorder is an interesting one that appears to be growing. I find the topic interesting because of all the headwinds working against someone being in complete denial about their financial situation. There is so much information available online now. Many states require financial literacy courses for students. Topics such as insurance and credit scores that used to be difficult or impossible to gather accurate information on are readily available. So, it does not appear to be a knowledge issue with this disorder.

My experience leads me to conclude there are three main reasons for someone to be in denial about their finances. One, parents are overly involved with their kids today. They are helicopter parenting (which is a sure-fire way to wreck your child's future) and not allowing the child to learn anything about the true responsibilities they will face. This includes financial knowledge. Two, partners or spouses often have unequal input to the family finances. It is common for one partner to handle most of the responsibility. This leaves the other partner with at least the option of completely sticking their head in the sand. This is not a solid option, but technically it's on the table. Lastly, there are simply more and more American's struggling financially right now. It shouldn't come as a surprise to us the response by many people would be to ignore the painful reality. It becomes an emotional protection response. This doesn't make it right or helpful, but it does help us understand it a little.

Below are signs you might be suffering from Financial Denial or Avoidance.

- **Avoidance of Financial Responsibilities** – You refuse to check bank balances, pay bills, or review financial statements. Duh. This is the literal definition.

- **Minimizing Problems** - Underestimating the severity of debt or overspending habits. Rationalizing financial struggles.

- **Emotional Responses to Money** - Anxiety, fear, or shame when thinking about finances. *Emotional detachment or denial to avoid discomfort.* I believe this is the cause for many people.

- **Downplaying Consequences** - Continuing harmful financial behaviors despite mounting consequences.

- **Inability to Plan for the Future** - Neglecting to save for emergencies, retirement, or long-term goals. Focusing only on immediate needs and ignoring future implications.

Financial Enabling

We all know these situations. I have never talked to a single client who could not come up with at least one situation they were aware of where someone was enabling bad behavior through their continued financial support. I suspect you quickly had a person in your life pop to mind when you read it. Let's take a minute to look at the most common culprits

PARENTS. I wish I could scream this from every rooftop in America. For the love of everything, stop giving your children money to go do stupid things. Parents buying their kids cigarettes because "otherwise they will just steal to get them". Giving your grown children money to pay their bills when they refuse to work. Propping up grown children's lifestyles because they can't be bothered to be responsible. JUST STOP IT. You are not being a good parent. You are HARMING your child. Forcing them to go through a short period of discomfort to come out the other side a better and more responsible human is quite literally your job as a parent. Act like it.

Spouses. This often comes in the form of one spouse feeling bad for working too much. Instead of correcting that error and spending quality time with their partner they simply give in and let the other person spend the family into oblivion. The partner can develop any number of negative coping patterns (drugs, shopping, gambling etc.), but the spouse finds giving them money and gifts easier to do than fixing the underlying issues. Again, STOP IT. It's not real love to allow your partner to self-destruct with your money, dummy.

How do you know if you have crossed the line from support to Enabling? See below.

- **Excessive Financial Support** - Providing money, paying bills, or covering expenses for others, even when not sustainable or necessary.

- **Sacrificing Personal Financial Stability** - Neglecting personal needs, savings, or long-term goals to support others financially. Accumulating debt or financial stress as a result of the enabling.

- **Being a Stupid Person** (My own title) - Encouraging or allowing the recipient to rely on financial help rather than becoming self-sufficient. Fostering a cycle of dependency that INHIBITS the recipient's growth.

- **Emotional or Psychological Manipulation** - Guilt, fear, or desire to avoid conflict driving the financial support. Using financial gifts to gain approval, control, or maintain a sense of importance in relationships. Gross.

Financial Enmeshment

Our next disorder is the ugly stepbrother of the one directly above. This is once again parents being terrible parents. Let me lay out some basics on steps I took to give my children some guidance on money.

Your children need to learn money. This is best done through the use of their OWN money with growing responsibility over time as they age. It starts with allowances and report card rewards or something of that nature. They earn small amounts they can then spend on small things they want. As they age, the amounts get larger, and the responsibilities grow with it. Teenagers get jobs (ahem...teenagers GET JOBS) and then begin paying for their car insurance. On and on with this small release strategy as they grow. There are entire books on how to educate your children at different stages of life about money.

Now notice what I did not include in my statements above. There was no mention of the parents' finances at all. That's because kids shouldn't be included in the financial discussions of their parents. There are numerous reasons for this. First, the children lack context and understanding of the larger picture, so the information won't make sense to them. Second, if it's a challenging financial situation the parent is adding stress to the child for something they literally can't do anything about. Lastly, it gives the child an incorrect belief they are equal in the household. They aren't. They're kids.

All of this said, it is important to understand what CAN be discussed with children assuming they are an appropriate age and can mentally handle the topic. You are welcome to have a discussion with your children about the process you went through to decide on the car you purchased. What steps did you have to take to buy your house? How did you go about deciding the bank you use and what does each account accomplish? How often do you check your credit score (and if it's really good, explain how you earned it)? These types of questions allow the child to learn about money without being drawn into your specifics, which simply aren't any of their business.

If you are doing any of the below things.....I think you know where this is headed. STOP IT.

- **Blurred Financial Boundaries** - Joint finances without clear agreements or shared accountability.

PARENTS OVER INVOLVING THEIR CHILDREN IN FINANCIAL MATTERS.

- **Emotional Ties to Money** - Viewing money as a tool for control, validation, or obligation in the relationship. Emotional manipulation is tied to financial support or decision-making. This is a person weaponizing money.

- **Creating Dependence** - Dependents remaining financially reliant far beyond what is reasonable or necessary.

- **Lack of Financial Independence** - One or both parties are unable to make autonomous financial decisions without input from the other. My brain breaks when I hear an adult say they changed their mind on a purchase like what new car to buy because their child likes a different one. I'm sorry, how much of the payment are you making? That's the percentage of vote you get buddy.

Financial Infidelity

Our last disorder is the secret killer. Financial Infidelity is so destructive because it not only destroys the finances of a relationship, but also the trust. I find this disorder one of the hardest for me to hear a client or friend confess to. I cringe inside because I know they don't realize the true ramifications of what they are doing. They believe it's only a money issue. Sure, it might not be a significant amount of money and maybe the family can afford it. It might not ever do any real financial damage to the partner. The emotional damage, however, can't be avoided as easily.

Let me make this clear for you, dear reader. If you are engaging in this activity, YOU ARE LYING to your partner. Hard stop. Trust broken may never fully recover. Think through that clearly.

- **Secret Financial Activities** – A person is hiding purchases, debts, savings, or investments from a partner. Creating secret bank accounts, credit cards, or loans that are unknown to the other person in the relationship.

- **Dishonesty About Money** - Lying or providing misleading information about financial matters, such as income, spending habits, or financial obligations.

- **Hidden Debts** - Concealing accumulated debt. This often happens prior to marriage.

- **Financial Manipulation** - Using money as a tool to control or manipulate the partner. Making decisions that impact the financial stability of the relationship without mutual agreement. Weaponizing money is a betrayal of your relationship.

Chapter 7
Financial Therapy Options

 Man, the last chapter was no fun right? It's not exactly pleasant to delve into the severe financial problems our friends, family and maybe ourselves can face. The good news is we can now talk about the positive side of getting healthier. I say healthier intentionally because the disorders are about mental health issues. So, the logical solution is mental health care. This leads us into a discussion on the types of therapies available to improve our financial picture.

I want to start off by being very very very clear. This chapter is NOT about self-diagnosis and then trying to work through some therapy plan on your own. Just like every serious mental health challenge you should seek the guidance and support of a trained professional. Additionally, to be clear, I am NOT one of those trained professionals. At least not yet. I am currently working through another graduate program (see the section on being a workaholic) which will result in being a licensed therapist. That is how strongly I believe this topic can improve your life.

With all of that said, let's dig in. We are going to run through a handful of the most popular therapies. I also chose these for the variation and differences. I want you to see how varied and individualized the therapies can be. People deserve specialized treatment for their individual issues.

Cognitive Behavioral Financial Therapy (CBFT)

Our first therapy dovetails off the main thrust of this book. Finance is more than math. CBFT blends the principles of traditional cognitive behavioral therapy with financial planning. It aims to help individuals reshape their relationship with money. At the core, it's based on the idea our thoughts, emotions, and behaviors around money are deeply interconnected. To make improvements in our behaviors around money we will need to improve our mental outlook towards it. This can be accomplished through a few exercises.

- **Cognitive Restructuring** - clients identify and challenge negative or distorted thoughts they have about money. Then they learn to replace the harmful beliefs with more rational, constructive thoughts.

- **Behavioral Interventions** - Changing behaviors related to money, such as overspending, financial avoidance, or compulsive saving. This can be done through a series of incremental changes in a controlled setting until the client is able to increase self-control levels.

- **Emotional Regulation** - Helps the clients recognize and manage emotional triggers that normally lead to poor financial choices. This may involve mindfulness, stress reduction techniques, or journaling about financial feelings.

- **Financial Education and Skill-Building** – Perhaps the most practical element of CBFT involves teaching financial skills, such as budgeting, debt repayment strategies, and investment planning. It sounds overly simplistic, but if you don't know these things it will likely lead to poor decision making.

Solutions Focused Financial Therapy (SFFT)

This approach is one I have often seen work well with younger people who have not reinforced negative behaviors over a long period of time. It revolves more around goal setting and less on the past traumas or errors. For this reason, some people find it less emotionally taxing. One of the key elements of SFFT is fostering hope by focusing on what is possible, rather than getting bogged down by what has been difficult or challenging. This helps people feel more optimistic about their financial future

- **Strengths-Based Approach** - Instead of focusing on past financial mistakes or struggles, SFFT emphasizes the individual's or couple's existing strengths and resources. This allows a more forward-looking experience.

- **Goal-Oriented with Emphasis on Incremental Changes** - Therapy focuses on helping define specific, measurable financial goals. The goal-setting process is collaborative, and clients are encouraged to articulate their financial desires and aspirations in a way that is realistic and achievable. Clients make small, incremental changes in their financial behaviors rather than attempting large, overwhelming changes all at once

- **Solution-Focused Techniques** - Rather than dwelling on financial problems or past mistakes, SFFT prioritizes finding practical solutions to current financial issues. The therapist encourages clients to look for ways to move forward, focusing on what is working and how to build upon those successes.

Narrative Financial Therapy

Full disclosure, I find this therapy fascinating. It ties so well into the concepts of our earlier chapter on your Money History. This therapy focuses on helping you understand your financial challenges as part of a lager story about your life. It allows you to remove the negative emotions about yourself from the equation. You are simply reflecting and "narrating" the story of your past.

- **Understanding the Financial Narrative** - The first step in narrative financial therapy involves exploring how people view past financial experiences, their relationship with money, and how these perceptions have shaped their current financial behaviors. The therapist helps clients identify core beliefs about money.

- **Externalizing the Problem** – Next the therapist helps a client with "externalizing," which involves separating the person from the problem. This means helping clients view their financial struggles (e.g., debt, overspending, financial stress) as something external to their identity, rather than as a personal failing. By externalizing the problem, clients can reframe how their financial challenges are influenced by external factors (e.g., society, upbringing, life circumstances) rather than viewing themselves as inherently bad with money. This shift allows clients to take control of the problem and see it as something they can change.

- **Re-authoring the Financial Story** – In the last step clients are encouraged to define a new identity around their financial future. One that aligns with their values, goals, and dreams. For example, someone who has always seen themselves as "bad with money" might reframe their identity as "someone who is learning to manage money wisely and responsibly." This gives the person power over the situation and allows many of the negative self-thoughts to be brought under control.

- **Understanding Influence of Family and Cultural Narratives** - Narrative financial therapy can help clients explore how their family's relationship with money has influenced their own beliefs and financial practices. It can also include larger societal narratives (e.g., "wealth equals success" or "money is a taboo subject") which influence how we view our finances.

Systemic Financial Therapy

If you have heard the concept of System's Theory, this section will sound familiar. If not, allow me to quickly explain. In many cases, the best way to view yourself is as part of a larger system. This applies to all areas of your life. You are part of many systems all the time. Your emotions, power, standing, and personality are all influenced by the system you are working within. Think about how different you are at work versus home. You play a different role. There are different people around you who also play different roles. All this impacts how we behave and see ourselves within the system. This same concept can be applied to our financial life. We are all part of multiple financial "systems", and it changes how we behave with money depending on the context.

When applied to a therapeutic situation, a client is encouraged to reflect on the system in which they find themselves and to identify all the various components (other people) in that system.

- **Viewing Financial Behaviors Through a Systemic Lens** - Systemic financial therapy takes a broad view by recognizing individuals as part of larger systems, such as family dynamics, societal structures, and work environments, which influence financial decisions. It often explores how family history, cultural background, and relationship dynamics (between partners, parents, and children) shape an individual's money beliefs and behaviors. Systemic financial therapy also recognizes that cultural and societal influences shape people's financial attitudes.

- **Exploring Family and Interpersonal Dynamics** - The therapist examines the family's collective narrative about money. This means discussing how family members talk about and manage money. You can imagine the way the "system" treats money will impact the way you treat money.

- **Generational Patterns** - Systemic financial therapy looks at how financial behaviors and beliefs are passed down from one generation to the next.

- **Couple and Partnership Dynamic** - Couples often have differing attitudes toward money, influenced by their family histories and personal experiences. Systemic financial therapy helps partners communicate openly about money, understand each other's perspectives, and align their financial goals. It also allows them to be intentional about creating a system that reflects their values and thoughts about money. Parents or parents to be are encouraged to be mindful of how the system they are creating will impact future children. By reflecting on the systems they were raised in, they can recognize the powerful impact of this work.

Chapter 8
Cognitive Dissonance

"Money is numbers and numbers never end. If it takes money to be happy, your search for happiness will never end" – Bob Marley

Now that we have hammered out the mental health aspects of financial psychology, I want to begin our exploration of the brain's goofiness with a game your mind is playing on you. Cognitive Dissonance. This fancy sounding term is not technically a bias. Instead, it interplays with all your other biases. Let's start by defining this monster.

Cognitive dissonance is a psychological concept describing the mental discomfort people experience when they hold contradictory beliefs, or when their actions are inconsistent with their beliefs. The term "dissonance" refers to the mental discomfort caused by conflicting information. When we are faced with cognitive dissonance, we try to reduce the discomfort by either changing our beliefs, justifying our actions, or seeking new information that supports our existing beliefs. This process of reducing cognitive dissonance allows each of us to maintain psychological consistency and avoid the discomfort of conflicting thoughts.

It is important to understand you are fighting against this monster all the time. You rarely even realize you are doing it. For example, I am a huge Cleveland Browns fan.

Yes, I know, this is itself a form of mental punishment. Anyways. I am also a man who is firmly against the mistreatment of women (duh). As a father I would be livid if someone hurt my daughter (double duh). When my favorite team decided to trade for and then sign to a massive contract an individual who was known to be ......shall we say not nice to girls, my brain stopped functioning. I, along with most of the fanbase, began suffering massive cognitive dissonance. My brain was waging internal warfare between my passion as a fan and my morals as a human. I was forced to make a choice in order to relieve the dissonance. I could change my beliefs by either no longer being a fan or suddenly being ok with harming woman. I could justify my new concerns away by claiming, "well he's just a football player and not my problem as a human." Lastly, I could seek new information to break the tie. Maybe the women were all liars. Yeah, that must be it. On to the Superbowl. The problem is for many fans, me included, this resolution has never actually been achieved. I struggle to this day about how to feel with regards to my team. If you apply this idea to other areas of your life, say a spouse who suddenly doesn't meet your expectations, you can see the damage potential. When the dissonance persists for too long it can cause permanent mental anguish and damage. This is why it's so important to address it early if possible.

Now let's move this into the realm of finances specifically. There are many examples of this playing out in our money world. The most common remedy we tend to use is justification. Let's try some on for size.

- You believe strongly that people should invest for their retirement. You aren't currently investing for retirement. So how does your brain fix it? By making excuses. "The market is too volatile right now; I will jump in when it settles down." "I am paying off my college debt, I will start when that is finished." Blah blah blah. All excuses. Yet, all needed to let your brain cool down because you know you are failing to do something you hold as a belief.

- You buy an expensive electric car. You get home and realize maybe you jumped too quickly because the test drive was thrilling. You are maybe, possibly regretting your purchase. No thank you to that mental beating. So instead, the post-purchase justifications begin. "I believe in saving the environment, so this purchase IS actually aligned to my beliefs." "I will be saving a ton in gas (ignore my work from home status please Mr. Brain) so the financial impact is actually pretty small." On and on and on. Just to make the pain stop.

We humans are incredibly good and fast at this process. We must be to alleviate the pain as quickly as we can. However, it's important for us to recognize it for what it is. If we catch ourselves doing the mental gymnastics, we must slow down and ensure it's for rational and positive reasons.

One last note on Cognitive Dissonance. Our internal steps to relieve the discomfort can result in positive movement forward. Let's say your current belief is you are not a "money" person. You just won't ever be good with money. You are one of those people meant to live paycheck to paycheck. Sound familiar? Suddenly you get a good job with a nice paycheck. You find yourself around a new group of peers who all have money. Your brain is absolutely going to struggle to make sense of this situation. Your brain will make a choice. Either it will begin sabotaging your financial decisions, thereby returning you to the state of poverty that matches your beliefs, or it will change beliefs to acknowledge your new reality as someone with money. Either solution will solve the mental discomfort, but only one is positive. By fully recognizing what is happening in your crazy brain, you take control of the process and can actively choose to move in the positive direction. In this way cognitive dissonance has caused a positive outcome in your life. Learning to recognize and harness this process is vitally important to all aspects of your life, but specific to our concerns today....YOUR MONEY.

Chapter 9
Imposter Syndrome

Come with me to imagination land. You are driving your car to work one morning and notice a young woman running. I don't mean from like a bear. She has all the proper clothing and appears to be wearing official running shoes. She has her headphones in and is just cruising along the sidewalk. If you saw this scenario unfold and I then asked you what you would call that young lady, what would you say? Would you mention her age? Would you say something about her outfit? No. You would immediately call her a "runner". After all, that is what she is doing. Here's the rub though. Do you actually know she is a runner? Have you seen her running before? Is she on her very first run ever? Does she view herself as a runner? Are you sure she isn't being chased by the bear? I want you to think clearly about why you would label her a runner. It is based on one thing. She is RUNNING.

Why do I bring up such a strange story and what does this have to do with finances? Well, it's to help you understand and overcome Imposter Syndrome. This syndrome is an internal thought process of self-doubt and feelings of inadequacy. You see, one of the most common and problematic issues I run into when I work with people on their finances is an internal belief they are somehow not "money" people. This problem prevents individuals from moving forward in their financial lives because they simply can't see themselves as being financially successful. This syndrome is also very common in the workplace. Many people struggle when they receive a promotion because they are not entirely sure they are worthy or ready to assume the role. They feel like maybe the people above them got it wrong and they aren't as capable or smart as people seem to think they are. Let's move this into the world of finance and see if maybe this is you.

During my financial literacy course, I ask my young students to raise their hands if they are investors. If I am lucky there might be five hands in the air. I then follow that question up with another, "How many of you have an IRA or something like a Robinhood account"? To this question I might see 20 hands go in the air. In that moment I have an entire class suffering from Imposter Syndrome. There are at least twenty people in the class who are by literal definition "investors". Yet, fifteen of them do not view themselves that way. They are blind to the fact they have running shoes on, headphones in, and are currently running down the sidewalk. To every person driving their car to work and seeing them run down the street, they are an investor. Being an investor means one thing and one thing only, you INVEST your money. That is the entire answer. I have multiple advanced degrees in finance. I teach finance. I present to corporations on finance. I oversee finance for an entire division of a large non-profit. Do you know what all that makes me? Well, NOT an investor. The assumption from most people I meet is that I am of course an investor. While that is true, it's not because of my background or experience. It's not because of my academic training. It is ONLY because I invest my money. That's it.

Now to be clear, simply throwing your money into an IRA doesn't equate with being a GOOD investor. That takes time, experience, research, and effort. However, you can never become a good investor if you don't even view yourself as an investor in the first place. Once you acknowledge the truth of what you are and what you have accomplished you can begin the process of getting better at it. This applies to all areas of finance.

One of the main obstacles young people and those from backgrounds of poverty face is seeing themselves as having money. Even when the time comes, and they DO have money they continue to struggle because they can't see themselves as having money or being worthy of what they do have. If this is you, take heart. There is an easy solution to this problem. Accept the dictionary as true. Wait what? That's right. The only thing you must do to begin overcoming Imposter Syndrome is accept the truth of the dictionary. If you accept and believe that Webster (popular dictionary for you young'ins) knows what they are doing, then you can overcome your issue. Do you currently purchase insurance? Congratulations, you are an "insurance" person. Do you put money into a 401(k) or other retirement vehicle? Congrats, Mrs. Investor.

If you are currently struggling to view yourself as anything, be it a runner, student, investor, mother, boss, or whatever else do me a favor and look the word up in the dictionary. If you meet the definition of the word, THEN YOU ARE THAT THING. Now that you know the truth, make plans to get better at whatever it is. This is especially true with finances. Myself and other "experts" (ahem, gross self-promotion there) can help you learn to be a better investor, but only you can make yourself become an investor. It takes $1.00 and one transaction to turn into reality.

Part 3: Cognitive Biases in Personal Finance

Quick Primer

Before you begin reading through the various biases, I want to take a quick minute and identify what you will see in each chapter.

- **Brain Games**: Every bias in Parts 3 and 4 will begin with the same concept. I will ask you to think through a mental challenge. These exercises are nothing too crazy difficult. What I am looking for you to do is simply be honest with yourself. Give your initial gut reaction. Answer as if you weren't reading a book on finance that you know is going to set you up to fail. These exercises are all about showing you the prevalence of these biases in our thinking.

- **Tech Support:** Next will come the explanation on the technical side of the bias. I will do my best to avoid the lengthy scientific jargon (I promised no boring stuff). However, it's important to understand what happens when the bias is triggered. Otherwise, you will find it difficult to recognize the monster when it shows its ugly face in your daily life.

- **Mad Money:** I will lay out various financial scenarios where each bias is commonly found. This area provides two intended benefits. First, you will experience many of the common challenges that normal humans run into all the time with money. While we all live different lives, there are common denominators in our experiences. Most of us want to buy a house and car. All of us must eat and buy groceries. Most of us are trying to save for retirement. The scenarios you will see revolve around these and more common themes. This will provide you with strong grounding when you face these decisions in your life. Second, you will begin to understand the powerful way corporations are using these biases to market to you. People like me are often hired by marketing agencies specifically because we can manipulate the way your money brain works. By recognizing the strategies being used, you will be able to safeguard yourself against the onslaught of information coming at you every day, trying to convince you to buy something or try something.

- **Travel Tips:** Now that you understand the challenge you face, I will provide some everyday tips to combat the bias. It is one thing to understand the bias and know it is happening. That doesn't help unless you can do something about it. Sometimes we can even use bias to our advantage. (Larger starting pay rate anyone? Stay tuned, it's coming)

Off you go!

Chapter 10

Anchoring

Brain Games:

How would you answer the following question? Keep in mind this is off the top of your head. No research allowed.

"Do you believe the price of a brand-new John Deere, 48inch, Zero Turn lawn mower is MORE or LESS than $5,000?"

What did you answer? Did you find this difficult? Maybe put a better way, did you simply guess? If you are like hundreds of people I have run this experiment on, you likely have no history of buying this type of mower. You don't honestly know the answer.

Now, take a moment and tell me exactly what you think the mower costs. For example, if you answered the original question LOWER than $5,000 you might state the actual cost is $4,700 or $4,500. Go ahead and lock in whatever actual number you believe is correct. I'll wait........

Now that you have your number in mind, here is the correct answer. $3,600. Was that what you guessed? Not a chance. If you say yes, you are a liar. Unless you happen to already know the cost based on personal experience there is simply no way you got that close. How do I know

75

this? Easy, I "anchored" you to a number that was too far off from the truth.

Tech Support:

Anchoring is a cognitive bias that occurs when you rely too heavily on the first piece of information you encounter (aka. the "anchor") when making decisions or judgments. Once the anchor is set, it becomes the reference point against which all subsequent information is compared. The presence of the anchor will significantly influence the final decision, even if the anchor is unrelated or completely arbitrary. The key factor that makes anchoring so potentially powerful is the very fact that many times it is not set arbitrarily. When people are aware of the effect this bias has, they will use it to gain leverage.

The Anchoring bias affects various aspects of decision-making, including negotiations, pricing, and purchasing choices. When presented with an initial anchor, people tend to make their adjustments from that starting point rather than evaluating options based on their intrinsic value or other objective information.

The anchoring bias leads to suboptimal decision-making because we all fixate on the initial anchor and fail to consider more accurate information. The critical piece to understand about anchoring is how powerful the allure of the initial offer is unless there happens to be preexisting knowledge. Think about the example I opened with. If you happen to know, even roughly, what the price of a John Deere ZTR is, then my trick would have no effect on you.

Your brain would have immediately rejected my premise of $5,000 as even being in the right ballpark. If you were indeed fooled by the brain game (as I clearly intended you to be), it's because you had no foundational knowledge to build from. So, my initial comment was the very first and only piece of data your brain had to work from. It became anchored to my randomly chosen figure for lack of a better option.

Mad Money:

So how does Anchoring play out in your everyday life? We can walk through a whole host of scenarios to help you understand the power of the bias.

For example (as promised) let's begin our exploration with a salary negotiation. In many cases young people struggle to negotiate their pay rates during the hiring process. The employer will handle it one of two ways. If the candidate is very inexperienced, they may ask the person what salary they would like. The candidate, not wanting to be seen as greedy, will likely come in low. If later they discover they are being underpaid, it will be very difficult to change that initial request. They are now "anchored" to the first number. The situation can play out in reverse as well. Employers will often throw out a low salary number fully expecting an experienced candidate to counter. By setting the anchor low there is a high likelihood the final salary amount will be well below what the employee could have gotten had they opened the negotiations with a high anchor. According to some estimates, failing to be prepared and making the first offer in a salary negotiation costs employees nearly $5,000 in starting pay. This lower starting pay is then the new "anchor" for future pay raises meaning every year for the rest of your career (unless you get wise and change employers thereby resetting the anchor) you are likely to be underpaid. Over a 40-year career this equals a potential loss of over $700,000. ($5,000/yr, 6% interest, 40 years)

For our next example let's move closer to our original brain game. Instead of a mower, we are now buying a car. This might be THE example of anchoring. When you choose to purchase a new car, you are completely reliant on the information being provided by the other side of the negotiation. No matter how much research you do, you simply have no way of knowing what it costs to build your new car. You have no way of knowing what the profit on the car is or might be for the manufacturer. Instead, the only thing you have access to is the MSRP. Manufacturer's Suggested Retail Price. Read that again. They just made it up. Where did they get the number? From market research telling them how much they can get suckers like you and I to pay. Every car dealer knows buyers are going to want a "good deal" after some haggling. So, they simply "anchor" you to the incredibly high and not real MSRP. You go in knowing the car has a sticker price of $50,000. You negotiate FROM THAT NUMBER. Why? What is that number based on? Many trucks and SUVs on a car lot have over a 20% markup. Let's say the dealer actually paid $40,000 for the truck. You talk them down from $50,000 to $47,000. You feel like you got a great deal, but did you? The math shows you just got a 6% discount (3k/50k), while the dealership just made a 17.5% profit (7K/40K). In no way was that an equal result of negotiation. The truth is the car dealerships possess information you do not. This gives them an unfair advantage. The MSRP creates an anchor you are unable to overcome even if you want to. The whole situation is set up for you to fail.

Side note. Please don't get me started on car dealerships. They are legalized monopolies that only continue to exist because they make massive campaign contributions. They are not beneficial to consumers at all. Think about it. They are one of the only products we can't simply order online directly from the manufacturer. We are REQUIRED to pay a middleman. Wonder why that might be?

My third and final example of this type of bias in action happens at Kohl's. While I do enjoy myself some Kohl's, they have absolutely mastered the art of Behavioral Finance. You will see this store come up time and again in our journey. In this case, the scenario is straight forward.

You buy 2 identical shirts for $15 each.

-Shirt 1 stickered at $50

-Shirt 2 stickered at $100

Now ask yourself the following three questions.

1. Which shirt do you feel better about?

2. Why?

3. How much did you save?

If you are like everyone I have ever met, you feel better about shirt two. Why though? Ultimately you paid the same amount for both shirts (which in this scenario were identical in quality and such). The reality is you really want a deal. Kohl's is pretending to give you what you want. By pricing the shirt ridiculously high, it appears like you got a real steal of a deal. The reality is you paid exactly what they wanted you to pay all along. You got anchored.

Bonus note. The answer to question three is NOTHING. You literally saved nothing. You SPENT $30. Saving is putting money away for the future. Stop letting stores convince you somehow you are saving money by giving it to them. That makes no sense, and you know it. Don't make me come over there.

Travel Tips:

To combat the potentially negative consequences of anchoring and possibly even harness the power of it to your advantage, we need to revisit the above examples. What did they all have in common? Knowledge. One party to the transaction possessed a piece of information the other party did not. This gave them leverage to begin the negotiations where they wanted to. From that chosen starting point, any final answer was going to lean heavily in their favor. Go back and envision each scenario, but this time you possess the necessary information for an informed choice. The John Deere question doesn't throw you for a loop because you are aware of the actual cost of a mower. The salary negotiations are easier because you understand your true market worth and going rates for your position. The new car purchase is closer to an equal win because you know the true cost the dealer paid to obtain the car.

In every situation you are likely to face in your financial life, there is research that can and should be done. This one step will provide you with a tried-and-true counter to the anchoring. It will also allow you to quickly identify when someone is trying to pull this exact trick on you.

Lastly, if you arm yourself with the correct knowledge, it can even work in reverse. The salary negotiation will turn out very differently if you know the true top end of the salary range you are eligible and qualified for. You begin the negotiations by asking on the higher end. They will counter of course and that's fine. The final answer will still be much higher than it would have if you allowed them to start at the lowest point first and tried to work your way up.

Chapter 11
Confirmation Bias

"Ever since I learnt about confirmation bias, I've started seeing it everywhere." – Jon Ronson

Brain Games:

If I asked you which country was the most important factor in defeating Germany during World War II, what would your answer be?

My guess is The United States of America. It would be your immediate and easy response. However, have you ever taken any time to research this assertion? Or do you simply believe the good old USA is just the bestest ever and of course made the entire difference in the war? You have likely watched many movies over the years depicting the U.S. as the hero country. We arrived and saved the day.

The problem with this assertion is simply, it isn't true. At least not in as clean a manner as you likely believe. The Russians would certainly like to have a word with you about history and their role in ending the war. Which, by the way, was a massive role. My guess, however, is you have never taken a single second to seek any opinion that counters your narrative of American awesomeness. This is the definition of Confirmation Bias. Also known as Selective Attention Bias.

*To be clear, The U.S. played a critical role in ending the war. That is a fact. It just happens to also be a fact that many other countries contributed as well.

Tech Support:

Confirmation bias refers to our tendency to seek out, interpret, and favor information that confirms our preexisting beliefs or opinions while disregarding or downplaying contradictory evidence. This will significantly impact investment decisions, financial planning, and overall financial behavior.

When people fall prey to confirmation bias in finance, they tend to:

- Seek Information That Supports Their Beliefs: Investors and individuals actively look for news articles, market analysis, or expert opinions that align with their existing views on investments or financial markets. They follow specific financial sources that consistently reinforce their pre-existing beliefs, avoiding those that present alternative perspectives.

- Disregard Contradictory Information: People downplay or ignore data that challenge their beliefs. We rationalize away negative information or dismiss it as irrelevant.

- Make Biased Investment Decisions: We are more likely to invest in assets or securities that align with our preconceived notions, regardless of the objective merits of those investments. This bias becomes dangerous because it leads us to concentrate on our investments into only a few asset classes. This in turn leaves us open to damaging drops in value due to lack of diversification.

- Resist Change: People with confirmation bias are resistant to adjusting their financial strategies or asset allocations, even in the face of changing market conditions or economic indicators. They hold on to losing investments, hoping their initial beliefs will eventually be validated.

The easiest way to picture confirmation bias in your head is every political debate happening in our country right now at the dinner table. Our country is so deeply divided politically, specifically because most people are living in an echo chamber. No one is willing to seek out opinions or thoughts from the counter view. Instead, they only watch the news channel that spews what they already believe. Reinforcing in our minds that we are of course correct. This is incredibly dangerous in both the public debate as well as your financial life.

Mad Money:

Examples of Confirmation Bias in finances are numerous. Let me give you a few cases where you might fall victim if you are not careful.

I will often work with young couples looking to get married or who have done so recently. We work to help them align their beliefs about money into a coherent plan they can both agree on. One of the things we discuss is always the household budget. Sometimes an interesting and challenging topic arises though. One partner will begin harping on a specific concern they have about the other person. Person A believes Person B is a reckless spender. I will be told, "Person B is always spending money on stupid things we have not agreed on." I will then ask for examples and normally the upset partner can provide multitudes of them. I then follow up by asking for examples of the positive things Partner B is doing for the family finances. Magically, that information is never forthcoming. The angry partner has begun the process of Confirmation Bias. He or she is ONLY seeing the information that proves what they are feeling to be correct. This is why the other name for this bias is Selective Attention. They are allowing their whole focus and attention to narrow in on the things their partner is doing wrong. If they were able to take a step back and give equal time and energy to identifying the positive things their partner is doing, they might come to a completely different conclusion. On balance their partner might be doing really good things for the family finances.

Our next example comes from the purchasing arena. People will often form an early opinion about a company or product in a certain category space. It might be a strong opinion about car brands, or athletic apparel, or brand of bacon. It doesn't matter how the opinion formed initially. The fact remains it becomes an embedded opinion for the individual. Moving forward every purchasing decision is going to be heavily influenced by those preexisting beliefs. This continues to be true despite any available facts that might run contrary to the original belief. To crystallize this, I will return to the world of cars. For many years, there has been a large subset of the U.S. population who refuse to purchase either Toyota or Honda vehicles. This is based on their initial belief these are foreign auto makers, and they want to support American made goods. Initially, this was a true belief supported by the facts. The first models of these cars sold in the U.S. were indeed imported from Japan. However, the facts have changed drastically since those days. Toyota is now the number one manufacturer of vehicles in the U.S. Yes, they build more cars in this country than any other company. Yet, many people still refuse to consider them. This has the potential of resulting in a poor purchasing decision where some options are being excluded based on faulty information.

Finally, let's consider investing options. Many investors begin their journey in the stock market with a small initial investment. Often this is in a stock they are familiar with and have some affinity for. So, the person decides to purchase 25 shares of Tesla. From that day forward it is highly likely they will only want to read or see news that paints Tesla in a positive light. If an article was to be published warning of a potential down slide in Tesla stock for some reason, the investor would quickly ignore the warning or rationalize it away.

"The author is just an Elon Musk hater."

"The author is mad she didn't get in early, and now it's just sour grapes."

"I researched that expert and they have only been correct about 50% of the time."

All these comments are perfectly normal reactions because in essence the author of the article is telling us we made a mistake. We don't like that implication. Therefore, we seek out data or articles that reaffirm our belief that we were right all along, and the author is a moron.

Travel Tips:

To overcome Confirmation bias, we simply need to be willing to admit we might be wrong. It sounds easy to say, but it's terribly difficult to put into action. You must actively seek opinions that run counter to your own. You must be willing to listen to experts from the other side of the argument. You must be willing to accept your previous beliefs might be based on factual inaccuracies. To provide a streamlined way of approaching this practice, we can lay out a 3-step process when making any financial decision.

1. You need to consider and admit there might be a counter argument or differing opinion on your potential decision.

2. Assuming you accept the premise of step 1, then where might you find the best example of a counter argument. What is the best source to challenge my beliefs and assumptions. Once identified, go do your research accordingly.

3. Lastly, you need to be open and honest with yourself. You need to be open to the idea of changing your position.

Using our Toyota example let's play it out. First, you accept your current beliefs about them only being a Japanese car maker might be inaccurate. Second, you begin seeking out counter points. You do a simple Google search on top manufacturers by volume in the U.S. Next you look at JD Power or Consumer Reports to see what their quality ratings are. Maybe you research which vehicles are specifically manufactured in your region of the country since that appears to be an important condition for you. Lastly, you accept you were wrong. The facts of your argument have indeed changed. This honest process now brings Toyota into your buying options. In doing so you are likely to come to a far better financial decision because you are operating in a framework where all the best options are on the table. You have not artificially and incorrectly removed a viable choice.

Chapter 12

Recency Bias

"Money doesn't change people. It unmasks them." - Unknown

Brain Games:

Scenario 1:

You currently own Apple stock. You initially purchased the shares for $15 each (prices made up). It has since climbed to a recent high of $35/share. However, over the past two weeks it has dropped all the way back to $28/share. How do you respond? What information would you like to gather before making your final choice?

Scenario 2:

You are watching the news and see your seventh story this week on violent crime in your city. You are not sure if you should be worried about the safety of your home and family. Do you call your insurance company to increase coverage? Do you spend money on a new and improved security system? How do you respond? What information would you like before deciding?

Both scenarios highlight our innate desire to respond based on the most recent information we have access to. We don't view this information as more data into a long stream of data points. No, it somehow becomes more important data. This can cause us to overreact in the moment and is called the Recency Bias.

Tech Support:

The Recency Bias is our tendency to give more weight or importance to recent events or information compared to older or historical data when making judgments or decisions. In other words, we are more likely to rely heavily on the most recent information we encounter, often overlooking or underestimating the significance of past data or experiences.

Influence of the recency bias includes:

- Recent Market Trends: We place undue importance on the recent performance of a stock market, assuming its current trend will continue into the future. As a result, we buy or sell assets solely based on short-term fluctuations.

- Recent Results: When we evaluate the success of a financial plan or investment strategy, we focus solely on recent outcomes, disregarding the overall historical performance. This leads to overestimating or underestimating the effectiveness of a particular approach.

- Opinions or Attitudes Influenced by Recent News: The Recency bias can affect public opinion and attitudes, as we are more swayed by the most recent news or events, while not considering the broader context or historical context of an issue. See everything in our current political environment.

Mad Money:

When it comes to exploring this bias in our own finances it is important to realize this is not just about investments. We will start with an example of the investing issue because it's so prevalent for people. However, I also want to highlight where this bias can go wrong in several areas of our finances.

Sarah is new to investing and has been considering investing in the stock market. She has started researching different stocks and their performance over the past few months. She notices that Jimmy's Wing Dings has been consistently increasing in value over the last few weeks. Excited by the recent gains and wanting to ride the JWD's wave, she decides to invest a significant portion of her savings in their stock without thoroughly researching the long-term trends, fundamental data, or potential risks. Three weeks later she finds out the company was part of a GameStop style artificial run up. The stock plummets and she loses a huge chunk of cash.

John is looking at a new home. He has been searching the real estate market and notices housing prices in his desired neighborhood have been steadily rising over the past year. He becomes so convinced that prices will continue to climb, he rushes to purchase a home before the prices go higher. He fears he'll miss out on further gains in property value. What he fails to consider, however, is the large number of homes going on sale in this neighborhood as current owners try to capture their capital gain. This in turn leads to a glut in the market and prices falling right after he closes on his new home.

Lisa currently has a credit card offering rewards points for different types of purchases. She recently received a new credit card that provides more generous rewards for dining and entertainment. In the excitement of having this new card, she starts dining out frequently and spending more on entertainment activities, assuming the rewards points she earns will outweigh the additional expenses. This decision ignores three factors. First, she ignores the fact her previous card offered better rewards for everyday essentials like groceries and gas. Second, applying for new credit cards is not a good thing for her credit score. Third, any rewards she does earn are a percentage of her purchases. She could have kept 100% of her money by not spending it on those purchases. She is simply overspending now.

Travel Tips:

The only true solution to the recency bias is to conduct more thorough research. Almost everything we deal with in life is cyclical. Trends simply come and go. If you want to think about this topic from another person's perspective, try imagining yourself as a ten-year-old child right now in 2023. Two and half years of your very short life were absolutely stolen from you by Covid-19. Everything about your world was horrendous for 25% of your life to this point. If you base your entire life perspective on recent history, you will conclude life stinks and is getting worse. Yet, empirical data is absolutely crystal clear that humans are living better lives today than at any point in history. We live longer, healthier, richer lives than ever. Our standard of living has skyrocketed over just the past one hundred years. If your ten-year-old self could extend your research and view back one hundred years, you would suddenly have a completely different picture of the world.

This very same logic applies to the stock market. I am returning to this hot button because it is affected the most by recency bias. I talk to people all the time that are concerned about the stock market. I ask a simple question, "Are you retiring in the next five years?" If the answer is no, then they are worrying about nothing. It doesn't make a difference what is happening right now in the market or what has happened over the previous five years. The fact remains, the U.S. stock market has averaged 10.36% growth over the past one hundred years. So instead of panicking about a temporary market drop, you should instead view everything as "on sale". If you go to the grocery store and chicken is on sale for 30% off, you don't assume chicken is over and it's time to find another meat. No, you buy a ton of it and stick it in your freezer for later. Treat your stocks the same way. If you loved Google long term at $35/share because you believe it's headed for $100/share (prices made up), and it drops this week to $27/share you should consider buying more and throwing it in the freezer for later.

Chapter 13
Framing and Reference Point

Brain Games:

Which of these two people do you believe is happier *right now*?

- Judy has $1,000,000 in her 401(k) but just lost a $100 bill.

- Dave has $100,000 in his 401(k) and found the $100 bill.

I think we both know which person you chose. Dave. He is over the moon because he found a clean Benjamin. Yet, he has $900,000 less dollars than Judy. Maybe Dave should calm down. Judy might also want to cheer up. She is a millionaire.

Second test:

You are selling your house. Your Real Estate agent comes to you with the results of the recent sale. Which presentation of your home sale feels the best to you?

- I sold your house for $175K, which is $10K less than you were asking.

- I sold your house for $175k, which is $5K more than your neighbor got for his house.

- I sold your house for $175K, which is $10K more than you would have gotten if you sold last year

I have asked this question many times and there is no one answer that wins out. Each answer seems to have an appeal to it for various people. Yet, what is the actual difference in these answers? Nothing. In the most basic sense, there is literally no difference in the results. Your home sold for $175,000. End of story. The rest of the information is meaningless. Your preference for one of them was nothing more than a preference for how the situation was "framed". This is what we are discussing in this chapter.

Tech Support:

Framing bias refers to how information is presented or "framed" and how that affects a person's perceptions and decisions. The way information is framed can influence the choices people make, even if the underlying information or options remain the same. Framing can emphasize either the potential gains or the potential losses associated with a decision, leading individuals to make different choices based on the positive or negative framing of the same information. It's simply the glass half full or half empty bias.

Along with the Framing bias we have an interwoven concept known as reference point. Your reference point is a standard or point of comparison that you use to evaluate outcomes or make decisions. It serves as a baseline against which people assess gains or losses. The reference point can be subjective and vary from person to person, depending on their unique experiences, expectations, and initial circumstances. When making decisions, people are influenced by whether an outcome is perceived as a gain or a loss relative to their reference point. The same objective outcome can be viewed differently depending on the context or reference point used in the evaluation.

These two pieces combine to create a strange situation where multiple people are viewing the exact same set of data, and yet coming to wildly different conclusions. In truth the entire idea of "good" and "bad" in most financial situations is nothing more than a framing and reference point discussion. If you were offered a job making $100k a year, would that be good? I have no idea. What do you make now? That would determine whether you believe it is a good thing or not. The same would go for me. Yet, we were technically offered the same dollar amount. It doesn't carry any intrinsic "good" or "bad".

Mad Money:

Let's look at some scenarios. Keep in mind as you review these, that the underlying information is the exact same. Yet, you will personally feel a strange pull towards one of the outcomes.

Consider an investment described as having a 70% success rate. If this investment is framed positively as "70% of clients see growth," people are more likely to perceive it as a favorable option. Conversely, if it is framed negatively as "30% of investors lost their butt," people will perceive it as a less desirable option, despite the identical underlying success rate.

How about we change and look at your stock purchase. If your reference point is the original purchase price of a stock, you will perceive a subsequent price increase as a gain and be more inclined to sell and take the profit. On the other hand, if your reference point is the stock's recent peak price, you may perceive the current lower price as a loss and hold onto the stock in hopes of it rebounding. Today's stock price did not change.

My final example comes from a popular game show. Deal or No Deal. The rules don't matter for our discussion but let me lay out the basic premise. As the game moves along the contestant takes on increasingly higher rates of risk in an attempt to drive up the "offer" from a fake banker. At any time, they can walk away and take the most recent offer. Conversely, they can reject the offer and move to the next round, thereby increasing the risk/reward cycle. Now, there are three ways to look at this situation. You could view your current offer as a comparison to your most recent offer. You could view your offer against the maximum you can win ($1,000,000). Lastly, you can view your offer against the $0 you brought into the game, thereby viewing everything as a gain. The finance person in me struggles to watch this game. I go crazy yelling at the TV. The "banker" just offered you $350,000 and you are telling me, "I came here with nothing, so I have nothing to lose". What? I mean WHAT? You have $350,000 IN YOUR HAND right now. Just walk away. The issue is this contestant and I are using completely different reference points. *Side note, my wife is always on the side of the contestant. She is apparently a wild-eyed gambler, and I can never let her visit Las Vegas unsupervised.

Travel Tips:

By now you have likely guessed what the solution to this bias is. You must learn to identify both your personal reference point as well as the true underlying statistics. This means being able to take a cold hard look at the math and the percentages. Dig into the facts and avoid the hype. You need to understand the reality of the situation, not the way you would prefer to look at it.

I also want to provide a word of caution here. Many salespeople in all fields know this bias is powerful. They use it to leverage you into a deal you might not otherwise accept. Back to our shady car dealers. When you arrive on the lot, the first question they will always ask is what payment you are looking for. Never give them this information. The problem is that as a finance person I can get you into a Lamborghini for $500 a month if you need me to. It will be a 65-year loan, but it can be done. Every time a salesman presents you with an option, they are reading your reaction. If they notice you didn't respond as they hoped, they will change ever so slightly to another approach. You are planning on car A. Salesman wants you to buy car B, but it costs $5,000 more. If he comes out and tries to sell you on the $5,000 increase, you will of course balk. If, on the other hand, he sells you on the difference in monthly payment it becomes more likely you might bite. The money difference in those payments over a 6-year car loan (which you should not do btw) is only about $80. Suddenly that better car seems attainable. Don't be fooled. It's the SAME $5,000 increase. It has simply been reframed. If I jumped in and said, "Hold on, your original payment was $400 and now it's $480, that's an increase of 20%", would you still be so eager to make the jump? I simply reframed it again. Watch out for these types of situations.

Chapter 14
Authority Bias

Brain Games:

First Scenario

- Who is the smartest person you know?
- What are they specifically trained and knowledgeable in?
- Last question. Would you trust that person to give you general advice on something like oh I don't know, investments?

Second scenario.

If you were reading a book written by some yahoo you have never met, but he gave you a bunch of credentials (like maybe multiple graduate degrees, college professor, and job as finance director) would you take this person at his word he was knowledgeable on the topic? Would you trust what the book says?

My guess is your answer to the final question in both cases is Yes. As humans we are aware of two things. First, we don't and can't know everything. At some point we will need to rely on experts to provide some quick answers for us. Second, we have limited time to fact check everything coming our way. Again, we need experts to give us the shortcut. This is the Authority Bias and man does it do a number on us sometimes.

Tech Support:

The Authority Bias involves placing unwarranted trust or reliance on the opinions, and decisions of authority figures or experts. It occurs when we assume the information or instructions provided by someone perceived as an authority are accurate and reliable without critically evaluating the evidence or expertise behind the claims.

This bias can influence various aspects of decision-making and behavior:

- Accepting Information Without Questioning: When presented with information from an authority figure, we are more likely to accept it as true without independently verifying its accuracy or considering alternative viewpoints.

- Transfer of Expertise: This impact is like the Halo Effect discussed in another chapter. When we view someone as an expert in one area, we tend to believe them on multiple topics without considering whether they are qualified in the second topic area.

- Influence on Purchasing Decisions: We might be swayed to purchase products or services based on endorsements from authority figures, such as celebrities or well-known personalities, without critically assessing the product's merits. Every company ever has used this against us.

- Trust in Misleading or Inaccurate Information: If an authority figure disseminates misleading or false information, people will trust and promote the information without fact-checking. Ahem, see the entire 2020 Election.

Mad Money:

Goodness I could go in hundreds of different directions with examples for this bias. We all know this is happening every day in our lives. For the sake of discussion let's stick to the examples that potentially impact our money.

The most aggravating use of authority bias for me personally is celebrity endorsements. These feel so transparent and obviously fake. Yet, they continue to work wonders for companies. We are convinced all the time that we desperately need a new product because some famous person tells us we do. For a moment, think about this. Does it make any sense at all? How could this person possibly know what is best for our lives? It can be especially egregious when the endorsement is for a product the person would have zero knowledge or experience with. For example, Lebron James endorses Nike shoes. Makes sense since he plays hundreds of basketball games a year. If the shoe is good enough for him to play basketball in, it's likely good enough for my old man rec league. However, he also endorses Kia. Get right out of here. There is less than a 0% chance he is driving a Kia. That is just insulting.

These endorsements can have harmful effects on your finances as well. There were multiple celebrities (Matt Damon an actor, Tom Brady a ball thrower, and Steph Curry another ball thrower) who did TV commercials for FTX Crypto exchange. They promised they would put all their money in the company, and you should too. The problem? The company was a fraud and went bankrupt overnight. Why are we trusting morons with no financial training for our money decisions?

The other time this bias can show its ugly face is with so called "expert" finance wizards on TV. People like Jim Cramer (complete idiot who just yells for an hour and is never right) and Dave Ramsey (being sued in a class action because of his support of a shady time share relief company) give daily advice to millions of listeners. Why? Simple, they have a TV show. What makes them the experts? Nothing. They are reviled or simply ignored by most financial advisors in the industry. They give cookie cutter advice (Ramsey) and terrible stock picks (Cramer). The main issue I have with you getting any advice from people on TV is simple. They don't know you. They have no idea what your time horizon is. They don't know your financial goals. They don't know your income level. They have no clue what you are trying to accomplish with the current decision you are weighing. In this way, even good advice they provide to a caller could be terrible for you. Stop trying to gain your financial advice from people who don't even know you.

*Side note. I support most of Dave Ramsey's advice. He keeps it simple and is a straight shooter. It might be generic advice, but still worth considering.

Travel Tips:

This might be the easiest tips section I write for this book. There are three key things to remember here:

- People on TV are actors. End of story. They aren't experts on anything. Celebrities don't use the products they pitch to you. They are rich and buy expensive things. They can't possibly be caught using the same products as us peasants. Lebron doesn't drive a Kia. Kim Kardashian doesn't shop at Target. Meghan Trainor is not going to the Met Gala in Skechers. Just stop. Research your purchasing decisions and buy what you can afford and what is best for YOU.

- Never assume someone who is knowledgeable in one area is somehow magically an expert in other areas. Certainly, some people can be super smart in multiple areas. You can't just assume it though. Check and double check their credentials in FINANCE before you let them give you advice on it.

- Never allow yourself to be completely at the mercy of another person, even in finance. While I hope you believe you can trust me and the things I write in this book, you still owe it to yourself to double check before you run off and change your financial life. Lucky for you I am not pitching some magic solution to make you rich tomorrow so you should be ok.

Chapter 15
Mental Accounting

"Spend your money on things money can buy. Spend your time on things money can't buy." – Haruki Murakami

Brain Games:

What would you be most likely to do with the following money?

- Money earned at your job.
- Tax return.
- Inherited money.

If you are like most people, you answered in something close to the following pattern. Your money earned at a job is used to pay for the things you need in your daily life. Essentially, it's your bills and such. The money you receive from a tax return goes towards a larger purchase you have been shooting for. Perhaps a TV right before the Super Bowl or something of that nature. The inherited money? Well, all the handcuffs are off for that one. You never planned on it, so spending it is easy. This money is headed for the splurge purchase. Massive trip to Europe, new car, etc. I do have a question for you though.

Why should any of these be treated differently?

If you follow a solid financial plan, it will include a budget with clear obtainable financial goals. These goals will be of different sizes and likely span over a few years. However, they are all part of a unified plan. Why would you allow your income to be broken into non-unified buckets? This is Mental Accounting.

Tech Support:

Mental accounting is a cognitive phenomenon in which we categorize and treat money differently based on the source, or purpose of the funds, rather than viewing it as a unified pool of resources. This behavior leads us to create distinct "mental accounts" for different financial resources, and we then manage each account separately, even if it may not be the most optimal or rational approach.

Key features of mental accounting:

- Separation of Funds: People tend to mentally segregate money into different accounts, such as savings, investments, or discretionary spending. Each account may have different rules or purposes for how the money is used, leading to compartmentalized financial decision-making. This becomes a problem when the accounts are not viewed in the context of a larger plan.

- Spending Rules: Mental accounting can lead to different spending rules for different accounts. For instance, some individuals may be more willing to spend money from a bonus account on luxury items than from their regular income account. This was the situation described in the opening Brain Game.

- Emotional Loss Aversion: We tend to react to losses in certain mental accounts more dramatically than in others. For example, a person would certainly not treat a loss of $1,000 in an investment account the same way they would treat the loss of $1,000 in cash.

Mad Money:

We hit on a few of the big-ticket examples during the Brain Game to start this chapter. So, we will set those aside. Let's look at a few other examples.

There is a common challenge that financial advisors run into when a client receives a large life insurance check. The person often feels like the money is somehow tainted because it comes from the death of a loved one. The client is often reluctant to spend the money as it becomes a strange but kind of understandable way to hold on to the person who died. In the most straight forward sense this is illogical. The person who died purchased that insurance so the client could continue to live their life with minimal interruptions. It was an act of love, and the money NEEDS to be used as part of the client's financial planning. Sometimes, the Mental Accounting is simply too strong, and their emotions won't allow them to integrate the money into their overall resources.

Another example I see involves a family's debt. While working with a client on a debt solution we will develop a payoff plan. Sometimes during that planning the client gets stuck in their head that this money is "allocated" to this debt. This money is "allocated" to that debt. They become so entrenched in this idea they struggle to grasp that perhaps moving some of the funds around and targeting the higher interest rates would be financially beneficial in the long run. The client has become so captive to the idea of seeing all their debt decreasing, they are resistant to making a change that would clearly benefit them. They have Mentally Accounted their money into different "debt" buckets.

Travel Tips:

To avoid falling into the trap of Mental Accounting, it is important you understand the unified nature of your financial plan. You have ONE plan for financial success. That plan may involve multiple revenue streams. It almost certainly has multiple goals over many time periods. You likely have different real-world accounts for different purposes. Bank accounts for paying bills. Investment accounts for retirement savings. Etc. Yet, all of these are part of the same overall plan. Therefore, it becomes imperative you treat all the money as equal in the plan. If you were not planning to purchase a TV this year, then a tax return doesn't suddenly give you license to do so. If you always set aside 20% of your income for retirement, then a year-end bonus gets hit with the same 20%. This is about being consistent.

The other piece of Mental Accounting you must be careful of is breaking your family finances into "his" money and "her" money. That is a recipe for disaster. To be clear, some couples have prearranged their finances in a way that makes it clear who the money belongs to. It's not my preference for strong family finances, but I can accept it if both parties are on board. What I am referring to is a family that has one bank account and a combined family plan, and yet the spouses treat the money and the spending decisions as different based on who is doing the spending. This is a nightmare. It will lead to fights and a breakdown in trust. This goes back to my above comment. Breaking through the Mental Accounting wall means understanding that ALL your money is the same. All your spending is the same. You are working on one unified plan. The inflows and out flows are all "flowing" from the same giant pot of money ultimately.

Chapter 16
Overconfidence Bias

Brain Games:

On the following scale how would you rate yourself as a driver?

- Far Below Average
- Below Average
- Average
- Above Average
- Far Above Average

How about your ability as an investor?
Same scale, but your ability as a house painter?

Most people have no rational way to judge themselves against the overall population on some of these metrics. Without this information we make an estimate. The issue is, for many of us we overestimate our ability. Badly. Btw, a national survey of the first question about driving found the following:

- 73% of all drivers believe they are above average.
- 80% of men think they are above average.

This is obviously impossible. 80% of men can't be above average. We are caveman dummies.

Tech Support:

Overconfidence bias refers to our tendency to overestimate our own abilities, knowledge, or the accuracy of our predictions. It leads us to have excessive confidence in our financial decisions and an unwarranted belief in our ability to outperform the market or make successful investments.

Overconfidence bias in finance includes:

• Overestimating Investment Skills: Overconfident investors believe they possess superior stock-picking or market-timing abilities, leading them to engage in frequent trading or speculative investments based on their perceived expertise.

• Ignoring Risks: Investors underestimate the risks associated with certain investments, failing to adequately assess potential downsides and the possibility of financial losses.

• Excessive Trading: Overconfident investors are more likely to engage in frequent buying and selling of assets, assuming they can consistently outperform the market or other investors.

• Overweighting Individual Knowledge: Investors overvalue their own research or insights, disregarding or downplaying the importance of external information or expert analysis.

Mad Money:

The Overconfidence Bias is a tricky mistress. It comes back to bite us over and over. There is a famous theory known as the Dunning-Kruger. This theory states that those least skilled in a specific ability tend to believe themselves far better than they are. The opposite is also normally true. Those most skilled tend to view themselves with less certainty. This is all relative to whatever is considered average. So, if you have limited ability in a specific field, you may believe yourself closer to the average than you truthfully are. This happens all the time in finance. I chuckle because in my experience helping people with their finances, I see this all the time. I will often have a conversation with someone about a financial topic. They will be adamant that while we have differing opinions or understandings, we are both equal in our standing on the subject. No, we aren't. Your three-minute Google search is not the same as my two graduate degrees. So, what does this cause in our financial lives?

The most extensive area Overconfidence Bias effects is investments. It runs rampant in the investing world. Everyone seems to have a secret recipe for getting higher than average returns. This ignores the historical fact that 85% of PROFESSIONAL mutual fund managers failed to outperform the index. Yet, everyone runs around thinking they have cracked the puzzle. This overconfidence plays out in investing too much in one area and failing to diversify your risks, ignoring the advice of actual experts and going your own way, and pitching your idiot ideas to those around you and infecting them with stupid.

The other side of this coin is failing to account for risks properly. Take the car driving example from above. When you believe you are above average as a driver you do two things. First, you buy less insurance because it won't matter. You are too good to get into car accidents. That only happens to losers. Second, you drive with less caution because again you are awesome. Both mistakes lead to financial losses that could have been avoided. The same thing can happen when starting a business. Your own awesomeness causes you to downplay the inherent risk in starting any business. Most small businesses fail. By somehow thinking you will automatically be an exception to this you are setting yourself up for failure. You need to fully acknowledge the risk and not believe you have some magic ability that will override reality.

Travel Tips:

Mankind has been trying to overcome this bias since the beginning of time. The first guy who thought he could wrestle a lion because he was stronger than average began this whole stupid journey. It is also worth noting here that studies show men are far more susceptible to overconfidence. Whether that is nature or the way our society has favored men forever doesn't matter. We are all  a bunch of hyped-up cavemen running around. So how do we begin to deal with this?

The first step is to educate yourself on the topics that matter in finance. For most people, when you begin to study a topic, you quickly realize how little of it you know. This begins to quickly stem overconfidence and shrink your head a little. The other reason to gain education in the topic is because it gives you a stronger ability to judge the true risks. If you studied investment theory, you would quickly realize the foundation of it is diversification. Any wild haired strategy you come up with that seems amazing in your head is headed for a disaster if it violates that foundational principle. By educating yourself you will realize this and change course.

The other way to keep yourself in check is to always run your ideas against the true experts in your field. I caution in another chapter about being too reliant on so-called experts. However, that doesn't mean a complete disregard for those who have knowledge on a topic. You should always seek the advice of those more experienced and trained in whichever topic you are challenged with. If you ask an expert for advice on your theory of investing and they laugh in your face, you might consider that a sign. You should specifically be seeking out those experts who might disagree with you. You want to know why they are on the other side of the fence. What are they weighing in their evaluation? This is always important because it's not about taking their absolute word. It's about learning to think through the issue in the same manner the experts do.

Chapter 17
Sunk Cost Fallacy

Brain Games:

What would you do in the following situations?

You are 3 years into a 4-year college program for engineering. You receive a call from a family friend who informs you that he has a job offer. It will involve completing a different 2-year program in management. Upon completion you will earn a salary of $100K, but you must drop out of the engineering program.

You begin writing an article for a popular blog. You have spent 6 hours of your time crafting the article. You then realize you have a totally different theme that might hit the audience harder and make a better impact. Do you throw out the original work and start over or stick with your first article?

You spend $40 on a low-end gaming mouse for your computer because you can't afford the one you desperately want. Three weeks later (past the point of returning it), you find out the mouse you have been dreaming of is on sale for $75, down from $250. How do you react?

Each of the scenarios above requires you to decide how much of your past you are willing to set aside to pursue a brighter future. If you choose to cast the past aside, all the time and money you invested becomes sunk. This is mentally painful.

Tech Support:

Sunk Cost Fallacy refers to the tendency for people to continue investing in a losing or unprofitable venture based on emotional attachment or the amount of time, effort, or money they have already invested, even when it's no longer rational to do so. Sunk Cost Fallacy is rooted in the belief that the past investments should influence future decisions, even when the objective analysis indicates that cutting losses and reallocating resources would be a more prudent choice.

Key features include:

- Emotional Attachment to Investments: People become emotionally attached to an investment because of the time and effort spent researching, purchasing, or managing it, making them reluctant to abandon it.

- Reluctance to Accept Losses: Individuals may avoid selling losing investments because they don't want to realize losses on their initial investment.

- Opportunity Cost Neglect: This fallacy leads investors to neglect the opportunity cost of holding onto a losing investment, preventing them from reallocating their resources to more promising opportunities.

- Escalation of Commitment: The sunk cost fallacy leads to escalating commitment. We continue to pour resources into a failing project or investment to "break even" or justify our past decisions.

Mad Money:

We can explore many situations where a person allows the sunk cost fallacy to take hold and damage their financial situation.

For some reason we continue to show loyalty and dedication to a job or career that is no longer optimal. There is an incredible comfort level in the known. We also struggle to accept that maybe we have wasted our time on a dead-end career for the last 5 years or however long. The problem with this thinking is the past doesn't matter. You will be employed over the next year one way or the other. The logical decision (all other factors being equal) is to go after the one paying you the most for your time. If that is not your current employer, then you owe them nothing. Would you choose them again if you weren't currently employed there?

Starting a business is challenging. Most of them fail. Most of those failures carry on far too long. You start out with an initial investment which absolutely includes your reputation. You are investing yourself and your image in the business. When things begin to struggle, we tend to double down on the investment. We pour more money into the business. We forgo other opportunities because we are so committed to making this new business work. There is nothing wrong with staying the course and seeing a hard project to its end. In fact, you won't accomplish much in life without this mentality. However, there is a limit to how far you should go. At some point you are choosing to pour money in not because you still believe it's a good investment but because you can't stomach the idea of failure.

I experienced this very issue personally. I started an insurance agency in my hometown. I dumped money into an office remodel. I paid for training, equipment, and marketing. I did ok for the first six months. However, I came to realize I was not at all built for sales. I hated sales. This is a problem in a career built on sales. Yet, I refused to give in because of everything I had previously "sunk" into the business. There was money and my local reputation at stake. At some point though I had to realize I was damaging my financial future by not cutting bait. I was never going to be a huge success in that industry and continuing to dump money was a complete waste. Eventually I sold my book of clients (for less than I would have dreamed of) and moved on. I lost most of my investment. It became one of the best decisions I have made.

Travel Tips:

The Sunk Cost Fallacy is so prevalent in finance because it has an extremely painful solution. We must admit we were wrong. We also have to possibly accept no return on an investment. Yet, it's critical we learn to accept these defeats if they mean a more positive future.

If you have a failed investment that has dropped from $100 to $25 in the last year. You have a choice. You can either look at the situation and get stuck on the loss. In doing so you will try everything to recover that money. This ignores the reality of the money already being gone. Your other (and correct) choice is to realize you have $25. If someone handed you a new $25, what would you do with it right now based on the information you currently possess? That's the only question you need to answer. If you can honestly (no BS'ing yourself) say you would put the new $25 back into the failed investment, then so be it. However, if there is even one other investment out there you feel would grow the money better moving forward than you have your answer. Pull the money, eat the loss, and move on. Otherwise, you risk the $25 being gone this time next year. What good would your pride have done you?

To avoid the sunk cost fallacy, you MUST make decisions based on objective analysis of future prospects rather than past investments. Being willing to cut losses and reallocate resources based on current market conditions leads to more rational and successful financial decisions. The question you should ask for every investment you have is, "would I do this again right now?"

Chapter 18
Availability Bias

"Lottery: A tax on people who are bad at math." –
Ambrose Bierce

Brain Games:

Scenario 1:

- If you were going to invest in a new stock this week, which would it be? Where did you get your information on the company? What was the main factor in convincing you it would be a good investment?

Scenario 2:

- What is the most profitable sport in the world?

Scenario 3:

- You are bringing a new product to the market. It is the amazing Wing Ding and is incredibly helpful for people living in a large city. You want to begin with the largest city you can in hopes it goes viral. Which city would you choose to launch your product?

Now for some answers to these questions.

I don't know you, but I can almost guarantee your answer to the first questions was what we refer to in the business as a Large Cap company. It was likely some combination of Google, Apple, Meta, Tesla, GE, Ford, Intel etc. It is a company you can name off the top of your head. That's the whole point.

The answer to the second question is Futball. Not American football. That contest isn't even close. Worldwide soccer earns three times as much as our football. Stop being so American centric.

The answer to question number three is Tokyo, Japan. This is the largest city in the world. Tokyo has an astounding 37 MILLION people living there. In fact, if you were thinking about New York City, then you were not even going into a city ranked in the top ten worldwide. Again, stop being so American centric.

All these examples happen because of something called the Availability Bias. It seems like common sense, but we normally make our decisions on information that is readily available in our immediate surroundings. This isn't always good though.

Tech Support:

The Availability Bias occurs when we rely heavily on information that is readily available or easily recalled from our memory when making financial decisions. This leads us to give more weight to information that is vivid, recent, or personally impactful, while overlooking less accessible or less memorable data.

With the availability bias we find:

- Focusing on Recent News: We are influenced by the most current financial news, leading us to make decisions based on emotionally charged headlines rather than conducting a thorough analysis of the underlying data.

- Impact of Personal Experiences: We are swayed by our personal experiences with past investments or financial decisions, giving more weight to the outcomes we have personally witnessed.

- Influence of Media Coverage: The availability bias is exacerbated by media coverage, as certain financial events or companies receive more attention and become more salient in our minds.

Mad Money:

The core component of this bias is simply what information you have immediate access to. Keep in mind this does not mean accurate or reliable information. Bad information will be just as sticky in your mind as accurate information. However, even if we assume the information is technically accurate, that does not mean it is complete or shown in context. Let's explore a few examples where the availability of information can alter your financial plans.

Jimmy is putting his investment portfolio together. He wants to be informed about his decisions, so he has been watching investment experts on TV and talking with his friends who are current investors. He believes he has the

20 stocks he wishes to invest in picked out. As a final check he asks his financial advisor to run an analysis of his choices. Sadly, the results are not positive. Jimmy has picked 20 stocks from the Large Cap category. He is woefully under diversified in his portfolio and placing himself in far too much danger from market risk. It turns out the only stocks talked about on the TV were the largest companies in the world because they move the needle with viewers. His friends also weren't a help because like most people they only know the largest companies in the world. This happens all the time and results in people missing out on strong investment options simply because they, and everyone around them, are unfamiliar with the choices.

Bonnie refuses to invest in her company's 401(k). Her reasoning is based on her upbringing. She watched as her dad moved from company to company. Every time he changed jobs, he complained about being taxed on the 401(k) withdrawals and how the company took their money back from him. After years of seeing her dad get "swindled" by these retirement account things, Bonnie simply wants no part of them. The issue here is twofold. First, her dad is ONE example. She needs to seek out more data points before deciding on a retirement strategy. Second, her dad was obviously an idiot. The withdrawals were taxed and penalized because he wasn't smart enough to roll them over to an IRA. The company "took back" their money because he didn't stay anywhere long enough to become vested in the account. These are simple answers that a financial advisor, or really any informed investor, could give Bonnie if she sought out additional data points. Instead, she is stuck with only the information easily available to her.

Travel Tips:

Like many of the biases we cover in this book, this one comes down to research and multiple data points. The availability bias is so powerful specifically because it's easy. We all walk around with a large amount of information stored in our brains. When questions arise or we must make a decision, we always dig into our own database first. If an answer is found, we assume we are done. What would be the point of looking for more answers when we have one at hand? Obviously, the issue is our brain malfunctions sometimes. We store bad or incomplete data. Often, we don't even control what our brain decides to store. Maybe somewhere you heard New York City is the largest city. Your ears might have heard the words "in the country", but your brain didn't bother to store that piece for some reason. So, when the marketing question from the beginning of this chapter comes up you believe you already have an easy answer.

To overcome this mess, we need to ensure we are doing proper research from multiple sources and verifying their reliability. The larger the decision the more double and triple checking we need to be doing. We should not be using someone else's experience as anything other than a tiny data point based on an anecdote. That one coworker's experience does NOT deserve equal weight with a research study done on two thousand people over ten years.

The final piece to keep in mind is the role of the media. You must realize the media exists for one reason. To keep people watching so they can sell commercials. That's it. So, it should be obvious they want to sensationalize everything.

When it comes to your personal finances you should be getting very little to no information from the national media (by this I mean mainly TV). You need to go to sources that are steeped in the industry. Trade journals, investments magazines, or local financial professionals are all options. Just make sure you are casting the net wide enough to capture all relevant information.

Chapter 19
Gambler's Fallacy

"The hot hand is an illusion." – Daniel Kahneman

Brain Games:

1. You are hanging out with some friends at the casino and walk by the roulette table. The board next to the table shows results from the last 10 spins. Every single one of the past 10 spins has landed BLACK.

1. What color are you putting your money on for the next spin?

2. What percentage chance do you give Red?

3. What percentage change do you give Black?

4. Why do you think they place those boards next to the tables?

As you thought about question 1, did you immediately say RED. Of course you did. The universe is due for Red. Well actually you said Black. I mean look at that streak.

Black is running hot. No reason to jump ship until the streak breaks.

Then I started hitting you with more questions about probability. If you understand math chances you realize the next throw of the little ball has exactly a 50/50 chance of being Red or Black. The universe doesn't care about the last 10 throws. They have nothing at all to do with the next one.

The final question is the real one. Why do they place those boards there? Simple, they work. Whether you believed Red was "due" or Black was "hot" makes no difference. Either way you are going to be drawn to the table. You never intended to get involved but you were hooked by the seemingly important streak you saw.

Tech Support:

The Gambler's Fallacy is a cognitive bias where we assume random, independent events should "even out" over time

- False Belief in Pattern Reversal – The mistaken idea that past outcomes influence future probabilities. For example, assuming a losing streak means a win is "due," even when each event remains independent.

- Misunderstanding of Randomness – Failing to understand that probabilities remain constant, regardless of previous results. In reality, a coin flipped ten times landing on heads does not make tails more likely on the next flip.

- Bad Influence on Investment Decisions – Investors believe a stock that has fallen several times will inevitably rise soon, even if market conditions do not support this assumption.

- Psychological Triggers – The fallacy is often reinforced by emotional biases, like loss aversion (see later chapter), where people desperately seek a recovery after losses, leading to impulsive or irrational financial choices.

Mad Money:

The Gambler's Fallacy is most often found running around ruining our investment portfolio. I simply can't tell you the number of times I will hear from friends and coworkers about the trend of the market. The question is always something along the lines of "do you think the market is due for comeback" or " Man, the market has been way up this week. It's going to drop a bit next week, right?" These questions fail to consider the most important factor. The market reacts to new information. That's it. The market does not try to level itself out. It doesn't care what "streak" it has been on. The market takes in new information and adjusts prices on the stocks accordingly. So, I answer these questions with one of my own, "Has there been some new change I am not aware of in the company or the news?"

The reason this issue becomes so important in investment planning is because it runs counter to the basics of long-term investing. The whole point of investing for the future (in this case I am thinking mostly about retirement planning) is to leave the money alone and let the market do its thing. By trying to judge when the market will turn or is "due" for a correction you are falling victim to the mistake of trying to "Time" the market. The key to successful investing will always be "Time IN" the market. Jumping in and out of stocks is a sure-fire way to short circuit your progress. Not to mention drive yourself crazy when the universe refuses to obey the laws of probability you mistakenly believe you understand.

Travel Tips:

You can likely tell from above where I am heading with this advice. The simple truth is the universe doesn't care about streaks or something being "due". There is no such thing as fate. There frankly isn't any mathematical basis for "luck". When you are faced with a financial decision you need to consider the current probability only. This remains true whether you are considering a stock purchase or a new car.

The performance of the stock over the last week or whatever is irrelevant to whether you believe it's a solid investment moving forward. Please note, I am not talking about ignoring all historical data on a company and its stock. That would be solid research to consider. I am talking about becoming overly influenced by some recent trend that "must" be ready to change.

As for something like a car purchase, your direction remains the same. Let's say you go to Las Vegas for the week and rent a Chrysler of some kind. You have a good experience, and nothing happens to the car the entire week you are there. You go home and consider buying a new Chrysler because last week was such a positive. This would be a mistake. It ignores the long history of Chryslers being junk cars and gives too much weight to the previous 7 day "hot streak". You are still falling for the Gambler's Fallacy even if you didn't go to the roulette table while you were there.

Chapter 20
Choice Overload

" Learning to choose is hard. Learning to choose well is harder. And learning to choose well in a world of unlimited possibilities is harder still, perhaps too hard."– Barry Schwartz

Brain Games:

Look through the following list and tell me which 2 mutual funds sound the best to you.

1. Fidelity Contrafund (FCNTX)
2. Rowe Price Blue Chip Growth Fund (TRBCX)
3. American Funds Growth Fund of America (AGTHX)
4. Schwab Total Stock Market Index Fund (SWTSX)
5. Vanguard Total International Fund (VTIAX)
6. American Funds EuroPacific Fund (AEPGX)
7. Fidelity International Index Fund (FSPSX)
8. Rowe Price International Stock Fund (PRITX)
9. Dodge & Cox International Stock Fund (DODFX)
10. Vanguard Total Bond Market Index Fund (VBTLX)
11. PIMCO Income Fund (PONAX)
12. Fidelity U.S. Bond Index Fund (FXNAX)
13. Rowe Price New Income Fund (PRCIX)
14. Metropolitan West Total Bond Fund (MWTRX)
15. Vanguard Wellington Fund (VWELX)
16. American Funds American Balanced Fund (ABALX)
17. Fidelity Balanced Fund (FBALX)

18. Rowe Price Capital Appreciation Fund (PRWCX)
19. Schwab Balanced Fund (SWOBX)
20. Vanguard Total Stock Market Index Fund (VTSAX)
21. Fidelity ZERO Total Market Index Fund (FZROX)
22. Schwab S&P 500 Index Fund (SWPPX)
23. iShares S&P 500 Index Fund (BSPIX)
24. TIAA-CREF Equity Index Fund (TIEIX)

That was fun, right? Right? Let me see if I can help you out. Now give me your favorite 2.

1. Vanguard 500 Index Fund (VFIAX)
2. Fidelity Contrafund (FCNTX)
3. Rowe Price Blue Chip Growth Fund (TRBCX)
4. American Funds Growth Fund of America (AGTHX)
5. Schwab Total Stock Market Index Fund (SWTSX)
6. Vanguard Total International Fund (VTIAX)
7. American Funds EuroPacific Fund (AEPGX)

Do you feel like I took anything away from you? Likely, only the stress of too many choices. This example highlights the challenge we have when presented with too many options. We think we want it, but our brain actually hates it.

Tech Support:

Choice Overload is a cognitive bias that describes a conflict between what we believe we want and what our brain can actually process. Remember, our brains only have a limited amount of power each day. Evolution has programmed us to hoard it for critical things. Wasting it on a decision with a million acceptable options goes against what our brain wants. Here are the possible issues faced when we run into the Paradox of Choice:

- Decision Paralysis – the speed at which we can make decisions can actually drop to zero if we are presented with too many options.

- Anxiety – For many people the increasing number of choices results in increased anxiety. We can also end up having increased regret after the decision is made because we perceive a higher likelihood of having made the wrong decision.

- Decision Fatigue – Mental energy is depleted and all decision making suffers.

Mad Money:

Choice Overload is also known as the Paradox of Choice. It's called a paradox because we believe we want choices, but our brain does not actually want that. This can play out in several ways throughout our financial lives.

The first and perhaps most detrimental involves the opening brain game example. The way I presented the mutual funds to you is exactly how most people receive them when they enroll in their company retirement plan. You are given a giant list of 40, 50, maybe 60 funds to choose from. The company believes they are giving you freedom and positive choices. The issue is most people simply don't have the expertise to sift through that giant list. The result? They do nothing. They are overwhelmed and leave their contributions in the cash account earning next to nothing. No one knows this has happened because companies don't help employees with the retirement plan. Bad news all around.

We also see this bias play out in the car world. Yes, back to our favorite example. Except this time, I am going to give a manufacturer credit. Many auto manufacturers believe in giving their customers as many options as possible. They hope to provide the customer so many choices that every potential customer can surely find something they like. However, it often backfires. Customers find the choices overwhelming and confusing. They feel like they are being cheated somehow but can't quite put their finger on it. Honda has gone in the opposite direction. They limit the number of models they offer, and each model has limited trim levels. This cleans up the picture for the buyer and makes it easier to commit. It shouldn't be a shock Honda sells a ton of cars. They have done some of the sorting work for us.

The last example is a silly one. How long does it take you to watch something new on Netflix. If you are anything like me, I'm guessing hours. There are so many choices available, I find myself just scrolling forever and never committing to anything. Sometimes I give up entirely and just play video games.

Travel Tips:

Traditionally the best way to deal with Choice Overload is to have some prework completed. If you spend some time crafting your "must have" list before encountering the decision you will be able to quickly filter all the available choices. You can eliminate a bunch of them right away.

I use this technique when helping people decide on mutual funds for their retirement plan. I ask a quick series of questions before we ever look at the list of 50 choices. I want to gather information on their risk tolerance, time horizon, and all the other standard investment strategy stuff. This in turn arms us with an ability to quickly eliminate a huge chunk of the options available. By taking the list from 50 to 10, the client can apply more reasoned thinking to the final choice.

The same concept can apply in almost every decision situation. The more you can create filters ahead of time, the more processing power your brain will retain for the true decision making.

My last comment would be to begin this process of filtering with what I refer to as "negative" filters. They are easier to come up with and will also allow for perks or features you didn't even know you might want. Let's use the new car purchase for example. You could eliminate SUV's, Trucks, and Vans quickly as things you don't want. You might also eliminate certain colors. However, if you try to list the colors you DO want (positive filter) you could miss out on some cool new color you were not even aware of. Most of the time, negative filters will get you far enough.

Part 4: Emotional Biases in Finance

Chapter 21
Endowment Effect

Brain Games:

- Imagine you just purchased 10 lottery tickets for the $200,000,000 Powerball. I walk up to you and offer to purchase those tickets from  you for $15. Would you accept my offer? How about $20? If you said no to both offers, what price would it take?

- Now think about your favorite t-shirt. I have no idea what it is (or if I do, then you should file a restraining order), but I will give you $35 for it right now. Will you accept the offer?

These examples highlight the challenge we have in evaluating the true value of things we own. We always value them too highly. Then we get super-duper upset when other people don't agree with how awesome our stuff is. We are all suffering from the Endowment Effect.

Tech Support:

The Endowment effect is a cognitive bias that describes the tendency of people to overvalue items they already own compared to the value they would place on obtaining the same item if they did not already own it. In other words, people tend to attach a higher value to things they already possess simply because they own them.

The endowment effect can have significant implications in various aspects of personal finance and decision-making:

- Pricing and Negotiations: When selling items, individuals may tend to overprice them, assuming they are worth more to potential buyers than they objectively are. Similarly, when considering purchases from others, they may be reluctant to pay the perceived high value attached to the items.

- Investment Decisions: Investors may become emotionally attached to certain assets they already own, leading them to hold on to under-performing investments due to the endowment effect.

- Decision to Let Go: The endowment effect can make it challenging for individuals to declutter or let go of possessions they no longer need.

Mad Money:

The Endowment Effect impacts almost every transaction we might find ourselves in. For each transaction we are either the buyer or the seller and therefore subject to negative consequences of this bias. A few examples.

The most common example of this bias involves real estate. The reason for this is people tend to have an especially strong attachment to their homes. If you ask a seller why they are refusing to budge on a price, you are likely to get responses that highlight emotional attachment instead of financial reasons. They might claim, "I painted the whole house myself", or "the buyer doesn't understand how good this house is for a family", or "this was my parent's house, and I grew up here". None of these things means anything to the potential buyer. They have no attachment to the house and will likely paint over your ugly colors anyways. This creates a major issue for the transaction as the parties may not be negotiating based on the same criteria. The same concept can play out with cars. It is normally not as extreme, but it can still play a significant role. The buyer has enjoyed many years of good times in the car and is trying to somehow convince the buyer that THIS Honda Civic is much better than the other 500 Honda Civic's for sale.

The second concern with Endowment comes into play with investments. For some reason our brain becomes attached to things we own like stocks. When a stock becomes a loser in your portfolio it might be time to sell it and take the loss (Sunk Cost Fallacy). However, many investors are emotionally committed to the stock. It has become more than a simple investment. It somehow became THEIR investment. Normally if you ask an investor if they would rebuy the same stock at the current price, they will answer no. They intellectually understand it's a poor investment but can't bring themselves to sell it. This causes people to hold losers for too long and not diversify enough when needed. Even winning stocks may need to go if you become overweight in one area. If you think it's hard to convince people to sell losers, try convincing them to sell winners.

The final piece of Endowment that messes with our finances is all our junk laying around. Americans are now renting storage units to hold all the crap they refuse to get rid of. This is insane. We are paying rent on a storage unit to keep the crap we likely couldn't sell at a garage sale. This is all because we have a deep belief our stuff is incredibly valuable and everyone else would want it. Sorry Charlie, your stuff is junk, and you would be better off giving it away than paying for a storage unit. This is one industry that as a financial advisor I want to see go out of business. Just a complete waste of money.

Travel Tips:

I believe the best approach to overcoming this bias is awareness. This includes when you are the seller as well as the buyer.

If you are purchasing a major item (car, house) it would serve you well to be aware the seller is likely attached to the item in a way you can't understand from your side of the table. By acknowledging this you can prevent unnecessary challenges. If you are buying a house for example, it would not help your cause to comment on the decor. It will only serve to upset the seller and make them dig their heals in. If you are a seller, it is important to recognize the person is buying four walls and a roof. They can't possibly understand your emotions about the home and are certainly not willing to pay you for them. Since this can be incredibly difficult to do as a seller, it might be best for your peace of mind to hire a realtor. The realtor can handle the transaction without emotion because they don't care about your home the way you do.

The other reason to be aware of the bias is to better evaluate your junk. I can make this advice simple. If you believe your stuff is worth something, put it on Craigslist and you will find out differently quickly. In some cases, I have even recommended clients struggling with decluttering to visit some garage sales over a weekend. I ask them to make notes about the things they see. When we meet up again their notes are normally something along the lines of "stuff was crap" or "was goodwill junk they wanted too much money for". I then ask what possibly makes their stuff any different. Everything you own is more important to you than it would be to anyone else. All our stuff is no more than three days away from being garage sale level. Act accordingly.

Chapter 22
Halo Effect

Brain Games:

What do you personally think about the following companies?

- Apple
- Meta
- H&R Block
- Tesla
- Ford
- Google
- Pepsi
- Nike

Now a second question. Which of the companies on that list would you invest in? By this I mean which company stock would you like to own?

Final question, which of those companies would you buy products from?

My guess is your answer to the last two questions was almost exclusively driven by your answer to the first question. When we form an opinion on a company or product, it tends to bleed over into all our thinking on the company.

Tech Support:

Halo Effect is a cognitive bias where someone's overall perception of a company or investment is influenced by a single positive trait or characteristic. When we perceive one aspect of a company or investment positively, we tend to assume that other aspects related to it are also positive, even if there is no direct evidence to support this belief. We give them the benefit of doubt without any actual evidence to back it up.

Key features of the halo effect include:

- Positive Brand Perception: If a company is well known or has a positive reputation in the market, investors may assume that the company's financial performance and prospects are also strong.

- Celebrity Endorsements: When a well-known celebrity or prominent figure endorses a financial product or investment, individuals may perceive the investment as more trustworthy or lucrative, based solely on the endorsement.

- Cult of Personality crossover: When a company leader is believed to have delivered an incredible result, investors may believe this can be carried over into new ventures. This ignores the possibility the new company has no connection to the original successes.

- Industry Leadership: A company considered a market leader in its industry may be given the benefit of the doubt in other aspects, such as corporate governance or financial stability.

- Positive Media Coverage: Positive media coverage can contribute to the halo effect, as investors assume a company receiving favorable press coverage is performing well in all areas.

Mad Money:

We see the Halo Effect almost every day of our lives. In some cases, it can be justified, but not always. Let's explore a few different ways to look at this bias.

At this point everyone knows Elon Musk. He has built a cult following of people who believe he can invent anything and every company he touches will somehow have a Midas touch. His success with first PayPal and then Tesla has led people to believe he is invincible. Yet, this ignores a few key factors. First, he didn't invent PayPal. He was a partner in the early stages and parlayed that investment into a massive sale that made him instantly rich. He then PURCHASED Tesla from the founders. He did not "invent" the Tesla car. In fact, he was forced to bring in experts from the automotive field because he could not figure out how to get production quantity and quality high enough to sell the cars. Now Elon has moved onto Twitter. Many investors believed his Midas touch would follow him. However, this is problematic. First, even if you give him credit for Tesla you must admit Twitter is a very different business. His experience may not help him. Second, the same investors who have traditionally been die-hard supporters of Tesla (environmental advocates) don't care about Twitter. So, he may not be given the same leash this time around.

Apple is probably the best example of a company that has built the Halo Effect. This is a company that can seemingly do no wrong when it comes to their loyal customers. For many people there is one and only one criterion when it comes to purchasing a new technology device. Did Apple build it? This Halo is being tested more and more by Apple. The company recently released their first Virtual Reality headset. There are already several competitors in the market and most price out between $400 and $500. Meta got crazy and decided to release a "Pro" version of their headset and charge $1200. People thought they were nuts. So, what does Apple do? They plan to charge $3,500 for their new VR headset. Read that again. They plan to charge 10 times the competitors and 3 times the most expensive set on the market right now. That is bananas.....B-A-N-A-N-A-S. You know what? They will get it. People will buy them with abandon because the Halo shines brightly on Apple. (Full disclosure, I really want one because I am weak)

The other impact of the Halo effect on Apple is the stock price. They not only have the most loyal consumers, but the most loyal stockholders. They are the most valuable company in the world by market capitalization. Most investors could not begin to explain the logic behind the high stock price. They simply invest because, "It's Apple."

Travel Tips:

When it comes to the Halo Effect in your life, the primary word to remember is caution. There is nothing wrong with having strong brand preference. There is also nothing wrong with trusting a company you have felt met your expectations in the past. However, it should never be automatic. Every new product is just that. New. Each time you decide to spend your money there must be an evaluation of the options. This means comparing the actual features and the actual price. Not just defaulting to brand name.

The other piece of the Halo Effect you must be very careful of is any impact on your investments. There is often a massive difference between a company's perception with consumers and their perception with investors. The largest negative impact this could have on you as an investor is lack of diversification. If you intend to only buy companies for whom you support their product as a consumer, you are likely to end up with far too few companies in too narrow a band of market capitalization. The odds are extremely high you buy products from only the largest companies in the world. Apple, Google, Microsoft etc. From an investment perspective these are all very similar stocks. By allowing the Halo to carry over into your investments you are ignoring 99% of the investments available to you and potentially opening yourself up to major losses in a stock market downturn. My advice to you is to make sure your investments are evaluated on their own merit and not as a reflection of only your purchasing habits as a consumer.

Chapter 23
Herd Mentality

Brain Games:

- What brand of phone do you own? Can I take a guess? Let me think.......Apple or Samsung. Was I right? Of course, I was cheating since those two companies have 85% of the cell phone market.

- What was the last new stock you purchased? Where did you get your information about it? Did you do your own research, or did it come from an outside source? My guess is you simply followed the crowd into one of the major players.

- Why do all teenagers throughout all of history dress like idiots? (*Myself included)

The underlying answer to all three of these questions is the Herd Mentality. We follow the crowd. Every one of us.

Tech Support:

Herd Mentality is a psychological phenomenon where we follow or imitate the actions or beliefs of a larger group. We often fail to critically evaluate the information or make independent judgments. This bias can lead us to conform to popular trends, adopt consensus opinions, or engage in collective behavior, even if it goes against their own beliefs or rational analysis.

The Herd mentality is hard wired into us through evolution as a protection mechanism. Since the beginning of our species, we have followed the larger group to avoid being eaten by lions. Somehow, that same instinct has been hijacked and now we stay with the group and buy the right jeans to avoid being labeled a nerd.

Key features of the herd mentality include:

- Fear of Missing Out (FOMO): The fear of missing out on potential gains or opportunities can drive us to follow the crowd, even if we are uncertain about the merits of the decision.

- Market Bubbles and Crashes: Herd behavior contributes to the formation of market bubbles, where asset prices become overinflated due to collective enthusiasm, and market crashes, where panic selling ensues when investors start following each other to exit positions. See below GameStop example.

- Amplification of Sentiment: The herd mentality can amplify market sentiment, making trends more pronounced and leading to increased volatility.

150

The herd mentality leads to irrational decision-making and a lack of diversification in investment portfolios as well as overspending on trendy products.

Mad Money:

Do you remember the GameStop stock buying frenzy that happened in 2021? If you do, can you explain what happened in financial terms? My guess is no. It was a ridiculous combination of financial information, rebellion, and get rich quick craziness. Over the course of a few weeks, people became millionaires and then paupers. GameStop stock is not a strong investment choice for most people. In fact, the stock was trending down. Most huge professional investors and hedge funds were selling the stock "short" (essentially banking on the stock continuing to decline). However, for reasons we may never fully understand a group of small investors got together on a Reddit forum and decided to fight back against what they viewed as rich guys dominating everything. They began buying GameStop stock in waves. This caused the stock to begin rising. This is REALLY bad if you are in a short position like the professionals were. They responded by trying to buy stock (to clear the short sale) and cut their losses. However, this only drove the price higher. Then the wider public jumped on the bandwagon and started buying. It drove the price even higher. The hedge funds took massive losses, and the small investors got rich literally in a matter of weeks. It was insane and not based on one ounce of financial metrics for GameStop. This was the Herd Mentality gone wild. Alas, as often happens the tide turned. Many of the initial small investors began cashing out their newfound wealth. This meant the small investors who were late to the game began to see their stock price dropping quickly. This led to a selling frenzy and the stock bottomed out again. Ultimately, nothing about the stock truly changed. The company was still garbage. The entire saga played out as a herd rush both up and down. It made some people huge winners and some huge losers. Such is the danger of Herd Mentality.

The other side of this issue is product purchasing. Every American falls victim to Herd Mentality when it comes to buying products. This can cause a few things to happen. In the beginning the rush of people to buy one product causes the price to spike. Once the product is popular enough, the knockoffs get into the game and the price comes down. Finally, if the herd becomes too entrenched and one company dominates a market (Apple iPhone) then innovation dies because competition is squashed. This whole process ends up costing both individual consumers (higher prices) and society (less innovation).

Travel Tips:

What can I say about this? Are you a human animal? Yes. So, you are going to follow the herd. That's what you are biologically trained to do. That said, it doesn't mean there are no steps you can take to offset the concerns.

Number one, never get involved in any kind of investment rush. Whether we are talking about a hot new at-home business, a small stock that is "taking off", or a real estate market that is supposedly exploding. The odds are very high that by the time you learn about the rush, it's too late. The savvy investors have come and gone. They are now just making bank off the late arriving newbies.

Second, please stop getting involved in investments you don't understand anything about. If the story above about GameStop left your head spinning because of the terms I used, then you have no business being involved in something like that. I am not claiming you need to understand the intricate details of every single investment. However, blindly throwing your money at anything is a non-starter. You know better. Now act like an adult.

Lastly, let's all agree fashion trends don't matter. By this I mean all products. The latest and greatest will be yesterday's news in like three weeks. By sitting out just the first wave of rush to a new technology, some estimates show you can save 48%. Think about that savings over the course of your life. Also think about your view of other people. Do you really care if they have the newest generation of a product? We tend to believe we will receive more product praise from others then we normally give.

Chapter 24
Narrative Fallacy

"If you cannot control your emotions, you cannot control your money" – Warren Buffett

Brain Games:

What does every car commercial for a new SUV or minivan include?
- Perfect family
- Dogs
- Vacations

Is there actually much difference between the vehicles? Can you even name a key feature from the last one you saw a commercial for?

How about this one.

What does every Jeep Wrangler commercial include?
- Off-roading
- Mountains
- Mud flying all over

When was the last time you went off-roading?
Why don't they ever mention the awful ride and comfort of the Jeep?
What kind of person drives a Jeep in your head?

Tech Support:

Narrative Fallacy is a bias where we construct compelling stories to explain complex financial events or patterns, even if the stories lack objective evidence or data. It occurs because we want to find a coherent and logical explanation for financial phenomena we would not otherwise understand. We often rely on hindsight or cherry-picking information to fit the narrative.

Key features of the narrative fallacy in finance include:

- Post Hoc Explanations: We construct narratives after the fact to explain past financial events or poor decisions, attributing causality to what may have been random or unpredictable.

- Simplifying Complex Events: The narrative fallacy simplifies complex financial events or market behavior into easily digestible stories, making it easier for us to understand and remember.

- Emotional Appeal: Narratives often appeal to emotions, providing a sense of comfort or reassurance in uncertain or volatile market conditions.

- Ignoring Other Relevant Information: We fail to consider multiple factors that contribute to the financial event, focusing solely on the chosen narrative.

Mad Money:

The Narrative Fallacy plays out in every aspect of our lives. Anytime something is too difficult to understand or too complex to explain with simplicity, we humans invent a story. In fact, throughout history, storytelling has been our preferred method of communication. We simply don't like to accept ambiguity. So, we tell ourselves a story to fill in the gaps. How does this bleed over into finance? Let's look.

Most investors don't understand the stock market and all the factors that go into it. There are financial factors mixing with emotional factors. There is no person on the planet who can accurately predict what will happen in the market. In fact, the forecasting accuracy of "experts" is laughably bad. To adjust for this, we tell ourselves stories. It can be different for everyone. Some people claim the market goes up or down based on which political party is in power. This is rubbish and has no historical truth at all, but it's easy to recite and convince ourselves we have an answer. Some people tell themselves the market is impacted by earnings reports and pure financial performance. This is also complete nonsense. The truth will always be that the stock market is a multifaceted and complex mechanism. It is impacted by a huge variety of factors. Just because we can't understand them all, doesn't mean it isn't true.

The story telling also bleeds over into our purchases. We often find ourselves fooled by commercials like the ones I opened this chapter with. I am no exception to this rule.

I own a Tesla. A large part of why I own this car has to do with storytelling. First, on the front end I told myself I wanted to be part of the solution for the environment. It is debatable whether electric cars are part of the solution. Again though, that is too complex a topic to boil down to yes or no. So instead, I crafted a narrative in my mind that convinces me I am on the "right" side of history. After the purchase I also crafted a story for myself. A Tesla is not a cheap car. To protect my financial mind against any kind of buyer's remorse my brain was able to develop a story about gas savings and no maintenance. While both factors are technically true, I am not sure math truly holds up in my favor. Either way, the story makes me feel better.

The final way this fallacy plays into our lives as consumers is when we buy into the story already being told to us. When you think of every major "brand" of clothes, you are thinking of the story. There is a reason certain groups of people all end up buying the same types of clothes. Are you a young mother with kids in sports? Then you NEED an SUV and a Bogg bag. Why? Well because the characters in the story of your life have those products. We humans like to adhere our real-life self to the fairy tale self in our mind. If you tell yourself, you are a successful lawyer, then you need to drive a BMW to make that story real. We allow the internal character we have created to drive our purchasing decisions as we attempt to make that person real. It doesn't matter whether we can afford that character.

Travel Tips:

Fighting back against the Narrative Fallacy can be extremely challenging. As I mentioned already, humans are naturally inclined towards story telling. We love it and can't stop our brain from filling in missing information with a story. It is literally the way we are hard wired. That said, there are steps we can take to minimize the damage when we recognize it.

First, evaluate important financial situations for how complex they are. If you know a situation is extra complicated, then you can safely assume your brain is filling in gaps. If this is the case, you can take active steps to educate yourself and try to bring objective facts to bear. Once our brain begins receiving real information it will let the story go unless it has become too ingrained. So, the earlier we can begin this process the better. For this reason, you should begin learning at least the basics of all major areas of finance. This will prevent you from going down the path of stories.

Second, we need to accept we will make mistakes. It's ok. What is not ok is to make up stories after the fact to justify our decisions. We can't learn from the mistakes when we do that. I teach my students to always do an autopsy of purchases. Review the purchase for what process you used to decide on the product, what factors you considered, and would you make the purchase again. If the answer is no, that's ok. Don't try to rationalize it. Accept it and learn from it. Be better next time.

Finally, try your very best to set aside the nonsensical story you are always being sold on a product. Evaluate the product for  what it objectively is. Not what you want it to be, what you think it says about you, or what the company convinces you it will transform you into. What it really is. Crocs are ugly rubber gardening shoes. That's what they are. They are not (cool, good looking, something humans should wear in public) shoes that will somehow grant you access to the cool kids' club on brand alone. Would the $10 pair of knock offs really change the character you have crafted for yourself? No. They would save you $40 though.

Chapter 25
Diderot Effect

"If you don't get serious about your money you will never have serious money." – Grant Cardone

Brain Games:

- The last time you purchased a new phone, what did you buy to go with it? My guess is at a minimum it was a new charger and case. Did you also consider a new watch band to match the phone case?

- How about the last car you purchased. Did any little extras find their way into your world? Maybe new winter floor mats. Or perhaps a car wash package. What about different rims?

- Think back to the last time you purchased a new house or moved into a new apartment. What happened next? Be honest. New furniture, window furnishings, decorations, security cameras, or paint?

What do each of these situations above have in common? They all represent extra money being spent on items that were not part of the original decision. When you were debating in your head about whether to upgrade to a new phone your thoughts were focused on the features and cost of the phone versus the one you currently have. You did not factor in all the additional add-ons that somehow find their way into our shopping cart. This process is known as the Diderot Effect, and it can become painfully expensive to learn this lesson.

Tech Support:

The Diderot Effect is a socio-economic phenomenon named after the French philosopher Denis Diderot. It describes our tendency to allow purchases to cascade into additional purchases. When we buy a new item that is different from our existing stuff, it triggers a desire to upgrade or match the new possession, resulting in increased purchasing.

The Diderot Effect plays out a few ways:

- Spiral Purchasing: The acquisition of a new possession, such as a new smartphone, furniture piece, or clothing item, can trigger a desire to upgrade or replace other items to match the newly acquired one.

- Influence of Advertising: The effect is amplified by trends, as marketing campaigns promote entire product lines or collections, encouraging consumers to adopt a cohesive set of products.

- Lifestyle Inflation: The Diderot Effect can cause spending escalation, where we try to upgrade our other possessions to match the "style" and presumed level of our new item. (You can't buy a new Mercedes and be caught dead still using a 3-year-old cell phone. What will people think?)

Mad Money:

I touched on some of the common examples already. However, let me add some context to the danger. When you begin to account for the unplanned expenses that come with purchases your total costs rise quickly. For example, the average additional money tacked onto a purchase due to the Diderot Effect is:

- Phones - $162
- Home - $10,601
- Pick-up Trucks - $1,831
- In Ground Pool - $8,000-10,000

As you can see, these expenses add up. The average American household currently spends about $66,928 each year. This means if you allow the Diderot to increase your new purchases by even 10%, you could be losing out on $6,600 a year. This is giving away your entire IRA funding for the year to unplanned purchases.

Travel Tips:

The only way to avoid falling into the trap of the Diderot Effect is to never buy anything new again. I'm kidding. The real solution is to become aware of the danger and account for it. You must acknowledge the impact this type of behavior can have and then take steps to include the added expenses into your calculations. Sometimes that means skipping a purchase when you realize the true cost.

Sometimes it simply means adjusting your calculations. Let me show you.

The Diderot Effect is not always a bad thing. It IS always something you must account for. My wife and I are currently working through plans to build a new home on a piece of land we purchased. Part of what we are including in our calculations for the new house are the extras the builder will have nothing to do with. We know we will want new patio furniture. We expect to put in special-order blinds on all our windows. I am quite sure my wife will be wanting the in-ground pool shortly after we arrive. On and on. We have two choices in this situation. We can pretend we will hold off on all the new bells and whistles and focus only on the home. Or we can.... not be idiots (and also lying to ourselves) and just account for the added costs. Considering these added costs gives us two additional advantages.

We acknowledge we have a limited amount of TOTAL money. If we want these additional things then something else must give in the process. Maybe we scale back on the flooring options or opt against the higher-level kitchen appliances. In either case, by simply acknowledging the Diderot Effect we should be able to keep the entire project within our agreed budget.

The other advantage of accepting the Diderot Effect is forced savings and time restraint. Let's say the extra items mean we need to wait an additional six months to save the extra money needed for the all-in Diderot house. Some might argue to go ahead and build the house and simply wait six months to begin the add-ons. That plan completely ignores psychology. You and I both know, once we move into the new house all bets are off. The emotions and excitement will take over. We aren't waiting to start. By saving it on the front end, we can postpone until ready because we have no emotions involved. We have already agreed to save for the house. The extra couple months is just baked in.

Chapter 26
Self-Control Bias

Brain Games:

Which of these two choices would you prefer?

- $100 today
- $200 3 months from now

How about these two choices?

- $500 a year from now
- $1000 15 months from now

Now, if we take a closer look at the questions, we can see they are identical. Both involved doubling our money in a three-month span. The only difference is the timing of the events. The farther out we push the decision, the easier it becomes to choose correctly. People show a DISPROPORTIONATE preference for rewards that arrive sooner.

Tech Support:

Self-control bias leads us to prioritize immediate gratification over long-term financial goals. It involves a tendency to favor present consumption and spending rather than saving and investing for the future. The bias arises from the natural human desire for instant rewards and the challenge of delaying gratification.

Key features of the self-control bias in finance include:

- Short-Term Spending: We succumb to impulse buying or spending on non-essential items, prioritizing immediate wants and desires over long-term financial security.

- Under-saving for Retirement: The self-control bias leads to inadequate retirement savings, as we don't set aside enough money for our future needs, preferring to spend on current desires.

- High Debt Levels: People influenced by the self-control bias accumulate high levels of consumer debt due to frequent borrowing for short-term expenses or impulse purchases.

- Failure to Plan: We lack a comprehensive financial plan, as we avoid making concrete plans for the future, preferring to focus on immediate pleasures.

Mad Money:

I believe if we take an honest look at ourselves and what has held us back financially, this bias may be the best explanation. The simple fact is most of us are obsessed with the present. The American culture is one that celebrates overindulgence and materialism. We are so conditioned by advertising and peer influence to believe the here and now is all that matters. We can't miss a single trend, fall one generation behind on tech, or cook meals at home like a peasant. All of this has heightened a bias that was already very strong in humans. Looking back on our evolution, it makes some sense. For most of human history we fought a daily battle to survive. Any food or pleasure you might come across better be enjoyed today because tomorrow you might be a lion's lunch. However, this built-in feature is now sabotaging us as we try to live until 100 and store away enough nuts for the next winter. I do want to explore a couple specific areas where this bias is dangerous.

The first point to highlight is the lack of planning caused by only being concerned about now. This isn't even about spending all your money now and not saving. It's about not giving any attention to the future and failing to plan. Estimates shows that only between 30-40% of American's have a budget. This will end up costing you massive amounts of money in the future. Quick example. If you save up the 20% needed for a down payment on a house, you can avoid PMI (bank's insurance in case you default). This alone can save you almost $125 a month. Over the course of 30 years, ignoring compounding, this means a lack of planning cost you $45,000. All because you were so focused on the present you couldn't be bothered to plan.

The second issue with self-control is ever rising debt. It would be one thing if we were spending money from our bank. In that case we would potentially be giving up 10% (stock market average) growth on our money in favor of a new pair of shoes or a meal at McDonald's. However, the average American family has about $9,600 in credit card debt. This means we are now spending well above our bank accounts. This is directly costing us on average (24% national average on CC's) $2,304 a year in interest. So instead of earning 10% on your money, you are paying someone else 24% for their money. This will never work out for you in the long term. Repeat after me, credit cards are for rewards (points, miles, cash back etc.) not debt purchases.

The last topic to discuss in this section is something known as hyperbolic discounting. This funny sounding phrase is the technical term for us getting worse and worse at self-control as the time horizon gets closer to today. This is exactly what played out in the opening game of this chapter. When we are forced to demonstrate control TODAY, it is very hard. When that same decision is pushed into the future it becomes incredibly easy. The fact is you can't have the money promised in 15 months or 6 years right now anyways. When viewing that future money from today, it's all monopoly money. Since you can't benefit from it today, the self-control bias is deactivated. This is another reason it's so important to do solid financial planning for the future. Your present self has absolutely no issue committing future funds to a project because it takes nothing away from what you could consume today. For this reason, I would recommend making any financial decisions as far in advance as you can. It will remove this bias from the equation as much as possible.

Travel Tips:

I am going to make this incredibly quick because honestly you already know what needs to be done here.

Make a plan. Like today. Start financial planning as soon as you possibly can. This will prevent much unplanned spending and allow hyperbolic discounting to work in your favor as described above.

Stop using credit cards for debt. Duh. There is no way I am the first person to tell you this. Stop buying things you can't afford dummy.

Automate your finances. If you fear your self-control will fail you each Friday when your paycheck arrives, then make arrangements now. Automate your investments, bill pay, savings, debt payments etc. Take the decisions out of your hand. It is much easier to make a decision one time than have to fight yourself weekly.

Chapter 27
Optimism Bias

"It's simple arithmetic: Your income can grow only to the extent you do." – T. Harv Eker

Brain Games:

Scenario 1:

* If you were going to remodel a kitchen, how much do you estimate you would need to spend? Now, what odds would you give yourself that you are correct?

This situation is an extremely common one in America because HGTV and Lowes have convinced us we need to remodel every six hours. However, as a society we are awful at projecting the cost of these projects. Estimates are that over half of the people doing remodels in 2022 went over budget by at least 20%. So, if you guessed let's say $20,000 for your remodel, the odds are you would end up spending $4,000 more. That error almost wipes out your IRA contribution this year.

Scenario 2:

* You are twenty-five years old and working on your retirement plan today. As you run the numbers you decide to use 11% as your annual return. After all, you

are a great investor and that has been your return for the last three years. You plan to max your IRA each year. For this year that number is $6,500. You run the math and after forty years you will have a total of $3,781,869 (real numbers). What if you are wrong though and the market only returns 10% over those forty years? Now what is your total nest egg?

The answer to the question is $2,876,851. That overly ambitious 1% cost you $900,000. Almost a cool million dollars based on using an estimate that was too high and based on only your own history (see recency bias and availability bias). Your optimism will come back to bite you in the backside.

Tech Support:

Optimism bias causes people to overestimate the likelihood of positive outcomes and underestimate the likelihood of negative outcomes when making financial decisions. It leads us to be overly optimistic about our financial prospects and investment outcomes, often underestimating the level of risk involved in our choices.

Key features of the optimism bias in finance include:

- Overestimating Investment Returns: When we are influenced by the optimism bias, we expect higher returns than what is realistically achievable, leading to unrealistic expectations.

- Underestimating Risks: The bias causes us to downplay or ignore potential risks associated with financial decisions, leading to a lack of preparedness for adverse outcomes.

- Lack of Diversification: As overly optimistic investors we concentrate investments in a few assets or classes we believe will perform exceptionally well, disregarding the importance of diversification to mitigate risk.

- Long-Term Planning Biases: When times are good optimistic people are less inclined to adequately plan for potential financial setbacks in the long term, assuming positive circumstances will persist.

Mad Money:

I am an optimistic person by nature. So clearly, I struggle with this bias in my own life. I am going to blame this bias entirely for my fandom of the Cleveland Browns. Every off season I desperately want to believe they will be better next year. Every year they are trash. Sadly, that doesn't stop me from buying tickets and fan gear. When will I learn? Likely never. Alas. Let's move on from my misery.

Optimism is another bias that plays out most frequently in our investment decisions. We get caught being overly positive with both the projections of how much retirement savings we will need and how high our returns will be along the way. This causes a double cascade of possible negative outcomes. If our growth returns are not high enough, we will miss the overly optimistic target. If our target is not high enough, we will not be able to retire at the lifestyle level we were hoping for. The typical outcome from this is under saving. When we believe we need less than will be required and/or count on too high a return, we are setting ourselves up for failure. It is important to believe in the long-term potential of the stock market. It remains the best source of future wealth for the majority of Americans. However, that general optimism about the positive growth of the market is not the same thing as accurate projections of your needs. We can and should believe in great days ahead. However, we should plan like a storm is coming.

The other area people struggle with optimism run wild is their budget. Your good friend Emily has decided she is going to purchase a new home. Emily has been doing really well at work and believes a promotion is on the near horizon. In response to this she adds a few bells and whistles to her new home. She also finances the home with an ARM (adjustable-rate mortgage). Her belief is the possible increase in mortgage payments won't matter in the future because her income will rise enough to cover it. Emily is now setting herself up for a massive failure. She is counting on several things to go right. First, she must hope rates don't rise too quickly or too far. Second, her promotion must be official quickly. Third, the promotion better come with a sizable raise. Lastly, she better hope she can keep the rest of her lifestyle in check because raises tend to cause us to want to expand in other areas as well.

This entire scenario is what caused the mortgage crisis of the early 2000's. Far too many young people bought homes they couldn't afford on mortgages that left them exposed based on career plans that were at best happy wishes. When the bottom fell out there was no safety net. Rates began rising and taking the payments with them. The promotions didn't happen fast enough. A few people were forced to sell at a discount to get out from under the weight of the increasing mortgage. That in turn caused the other homes to begin dropping in value as underpriced homes hit the market in waves. When people tried to refinance to a standard 30-year fixed rate, they were unable to because their equity was negative from the value drops. So, people began foreclosing. The cycle was in full swing and crushed everything in its path.

Travel Tips:

My advice on optimism is simple. I will restate what I mentioned above. Dream like the future will be amazing, plan like it will be a nightmare. You need to build in huge amounts of margin on your investments and your budget. Try to consider what you believe to be the best projections of the future and then downsize from there. Lower your expected returns. Raise your required nest egg. Make sure your finances will hold up under the stress of being wrong by a decent amount. The really cool part about planning in this manner is the positive side effects. From now until the end of the plan, you will sleep better knowing your worst-case scenario is covered. Sleep is good. In addition, if you do reach the end of the plan and things have gone better than expected, awesome. No one complains about having too much money.

Chapter 28
Loss Aversion

Brain Games:

Think about your own reaction to these two events.

- You find $100 on the ground.
- You realize you dropped $100 on the ground, and it's gone.

Which event evokes a LARGER emotional response?

Now try this game.

- I am going to flip a coin 100 times.
- If Heads wins, I give you $500. Tails wins, you give me $500

What odds would I have to offer you for you to take the bet? Would you require me to get 55 Tails? 65? 85?

 If your response to was anything higher than 50, you are exhibiting Loss Aversion. We HATE to lose money. Far more than we like to win money. Seems strange, but you just proved the theory correct.

Tech Support:

Loss aversion is a cognitive bias where that causes people to feel the pain of losses more acutely than the pleasure of equivalent gains. It leads us to be highly risk-averse and reluctant to take actions where we could potentially see losses, even when the potential gains outweigh the possible downsides. This results in us making suboptimal financial decisions and missing out on profitable opportunities due to an intense fear of losing money.

Loss aversion in finance includes:

- Reluctance to Sell: Investors hold onto losing investments for extended periods, hoping that the investments will eventually recover rather than realizing losses by selling. After all we don't feel like the loss is real until we cash out.

- Preoccupation with Avoiding Losses: The bias can lead us to prioritize protecting our wealth and avoiding risks over pursuing potentially higher returns through investments. The fear of losses can cloud judgment and hinder individuals from making objective and rational financial choices. Being concerned with losses is not always a bad thing, but we can take it too far.

- Fear of Regret: Loss aversion is often driven by the fear of regret, as we anticipate feeling regretful if an investment leads to losses, even if the decision was rational at the time.

Mad Money:

Loss aversion plays out financially for us in several ways. Most of them start off being smart and defensible. As time goes on, we allow our instinct to take us too far down the path of concern. This becomes detrimental to our financial future when we can't balance fear of loss against the very real need to take some level of risk to secure gains. Here are three specific ways loss aversion creeps up on us.

Insurance is a good thing. You absolutely need to make sure you are properly covered for losses by purchasing adequate insurance. However, the extreme fear of loss can lead us down the path of buying far more insurance than we would reasonably ever need. Insurance is the stop gap against catastrophic losses. It is not designed to prevent or pay for every single little loss you might run into during your life. By trying to over-insure and cover all possible losses, you are spending money that would be better served in the bank or put towards investments. You must be careful not to purchase insurance for minor or highly improbable events.

Having a cash safety net is another positive thing for your financial life. I will highlight this later when we reach the chapter on Financial Habits. However, like insurance this can go too far. Cash in the bank is essentially self-funded insurance. It is there to protect you against unforeseen circumstances. This is why we call it the rainy-day fund. Yet, it's important to remember that cash in the bank is still technically an investment. It happens to be an extremely low interest investment. Cash almost never earns enough to keep up with inflation, so in terms of spending power you are losing ground. There is absolutely a psychological component of having enough cash in the bank that no amount of interest could make up for. Being able to sleep at night is a nice feature of a solid bank account. Just don't let this get out of control. Something in the ballpark of 6 months cash in the bank is plenty. After that you are letting loss aversion control your actions instead of good financial sense.

The final highlighted area of finance where it is difficult for people to overcome loss aversion is in taking necessary risks. We tend to view risk as a bad thing. That is not accurate. Risk is really the "cost" of a potential gain. For example, let's say you decide to go to college and take out loans to do so. You are taking on risk. There is a chance you might not get a job and the loans may be difficult to repay. Yet, the evidence is overwhelming that a college degree (if you get one in an employable field) greatly increases your earning power. That is a risk you SHOULD take. The same thing goes for the stock market. There is a price to be paid for being in the market. There are years you will lose some value due to market downturns. If you only focus on those possible losses and decide to sit out of the market, you are willingly giving up the potential for incredible growth over time. Again, being cautious with your money is a good thing. Being scared with your money is not.

Travel Tips:

You can likely tell from my example above where this list of suggestions is headed. In fact, I can really boil my tips down to one key theme. You need to take risks sometimes. Let's dig into the theme a little bit more.

Your first task to overcome loss aversion is to research and truly understand the risk-reward trade-off you are being asked to consider. Far too many times we assume the worst-case scenario. Often, even the downside we face is not as severe as we imagine in our minds. Conversely, we also need to understand the true upside. There will be times when the instinct for loss aversion is good. It will save you from jumping off the cliff. If the potential reward is minimal, then your loss aversion is warranted. You should only be willing to pay the risk "price" for a return that justifies it.

The second task I am assigning you is to reframe your idea of risk as a cost. When you purchase a product, you do so with full knowledge of the price. This allows you to decide in your mind as to the value trade-off. This is difficult with financial products because the cost can be hard to identify. You must become comfortable understanding that cost IS risk. Think about insurance. You pay a monthly premium for your car insurance. You pay a higher premium for each level you lower your deductible. By having a lower deductible, you are pushing more of the risk onto the insurance carrier. This comes at a price. In this case the premium. Anytime you are faced with a financial decision you need to look at the cost and mentally convert it to risk or vice versa.

The last piece of advice is straightforward. You need to accept a bit more risk than you are naturally comfortable with. You can assume the amount of risk that feels "safe" to you is being tamped down by the loss aversion. Most losses are nowhere near as large or painful as you initially fear. So, to give yourself the best opportunity for long-term growth you need to be willing to accept some moderate risks. This means getting involved in the stock market sometimes. This means raising your deductibles on your insurance to save on premiums. This means using some of the cash you hoarded (beyond 6 months) to invest in a higher yield product. Heck go wild with that cash and get a CD or something. I am kidding. It would be slightly better though. In any case, go ahead and acknowledge you are slightly uncomfortable with a situation. Then do it anyways. I am not asking you not to be real about your concerns. I am asking you to be objective and make tough decisions when needed.

Chapter 29
Utility

Brain Games:

1. You are lying on the beach and thinking about how much you would enjoy a nice cold Pepsi. A buddy gets up and offers to bring you back one from the fancy resort hotel you are staying at. He asks how much you are willing to pay for it.

5. What price do you tell him?

6. Does your answer change if there is a gas station across the street?

7. What price do you pay for Pepsi at the grocery store?

8. What about if you were attending a concert?

9. How about if you were out of the country and had not been able to enjoy your favorite Pepsi in a couple weeks. You come across the only store in the foreign city that sells Pepsi. How much are you willing to pony up now?

As you thought through your answers, were you struck by how different the amounts were? Were you also a little surprised by how quickly you adjusted your price allowances? Shouldn't this make you feel a little strange since I never once changed the product. Only the location or situation changed.

Let's try another game:

2. You are about to purchase a mouse for $50. The salesperson informs you the mouse is on clearance at the store's other location, located twenty minutes away. You want the mouse today. What would the discount need to be (in dollars) for you to travel to the other location?

3. Ok, now the exact same scenario but this time it's a laptop computer you are looking at for $2,000. Now how big does the discount need to be to make the drive?

When I run this quiz live, the most common answer to the first question (mouse purchase) is somewhere around a $20 discount. So, most people acknowledge they are willing to drive $20 minutes to save $20. If you fall in that group, would you be willing to drive if the laptop was $1,980? My guess is no. Why not? What is the difference? It's the exact same $20. So, something else must be going on here.

Tech Support:

In the context of personal finance, Utility refers to the satisfaction or value we derive from financial choices or the consumption of goods. This concept comes originally from behavioral economics, which suggests that people make financial decisions based on the perceived benefits and happiness they expect to gain from their choices.

Key features of Utility include:

- Highly Subjective: Utility varies from person to person. Different individuals may derive varying levels of satisfaction from the same financial decision or consumption of a particular product or service. Think about a new Coach purse. Does it excite you? I am sure it does for some and not at all for others.

- Utility has marginal impact: The additional satisfaction gained from consuming one more unit of a product or service diminishes as consumption increases. For example, the first slice of pizza may bring great satisfaction, but each subsequent slice provides less additional enjoyment.

- Time Preference: Utility also plays a role in a person's time preferences because we make decisions about allocating money between current consumption and saving for the future based on our perceptions of present versus future satisfaction.

- Transactional Changes: Utility for the same item can change based on nothing more than our situation. Location changes, type of business, and availability all play a huge role in how we view the same item.

Mad Money:

The idea of utility is something you must be aware of as it causes multiple issues in our financial lives. Try these on for size.

Depending on which data you review, money problems in a marriage are anywhere between the number one and number three reason for divorce. Regardless of which of those rankings you consider; money issues are a huge martial problem. Yet, more money doesn't statistically solve these problems. So, there must be something else going on. The answer is utility differences between spouses.

Let's say your wife chooses to get her nails done every week and spends $200 a month because of it. You choose to pay for a subscription to your favorite online game each month and it costs $100 a month. Every single month you both fight over these expenses. You can't understand why she needs them done every week. You also don't understand why she can't just do them herself at home. She doesn't understand why you still play video games like a twelve-year-old. Maybe try going to the gym like an adult. This goes on for months and nothing is ever solved. Now ask yourself a question. Did I mention anything about how much money the couple earns? No. Yet, you were able to picture these fights and realize it has nothing to do with money. These are value judgments. This couple could earn $50,000 a year or $500,000 a year. She still thinks he is being a child, and he thinks she is wasting money. No income change will fix this.

The next challenge with Utility is a transactional one. Most Americans are having their family budget brutally attacked by one criminal each month. Dining out. The amount of money being wasted on eating out is stunning. Notice I said wasted. As I wrote that word, I quickly realized I was expressing a vastly different utility. I don't value eating out at all. So, to me it is wasteful. It might not be to you. Either way, you are falling victim to Transactional utility. You are paying far more money for the same product based on nothing more than situation and location. Set aside the food for a minute. Arguments could be made that you can't prepare the same food at home as a chef can. I get it. The drinks though? You are paying almost four times as much for drinks at a restaurant as you do at home. The average family spends over $300 a month dining out. That equates to about five meals total. Think about spending $60 a meal at home. I am pretty sure you can see this is clearly not a financial decision. This is 100% a psychological decision. It is a situation where finance is taking a backseat to your life preferences. That is ok in some instances. I want you to live a life you love and enjoy. Buyer beware, however, when this is happening too much. Transactional utility (food, alcohol, movies, games, etc.) can dig into your budget severely if you aren't careful.

The final piece of Utility I want to address in your finances comes down to one word. Enough. Most Americans are buying far too much stuff. More specifically, we are buying multiples of the same product category hoping for some dopamine hit that never comes. How many shoes do you own? How many of them are tennis shoes? The last time you went clothes shopping, were you excited about the new pair of jeans? If you bought 4 pairs, were you 4 times as excited? We all need to be better at recognizing the marginal impact of utility. The first bite of ice cream is amazing. (*side note, this is my largest weakness. I need to see an ice cream therapist) The second bite is still good, but not mind blowing. By the tenth (or in my case 52nd) bite the effect is completely gone. We continue to pay the full price, in calories this time, but receive less and less enjoyment. The same happens with our money. The first jeans are full price, full enjoyment. The second jeans are still full price, but with far less enjoyment. At some point we are buying because we are trying to fill a psychological hole as opposed to meeting a material need. Stop it.

Travel Tips:

For the tips section I am going to use a quick hit format to cover a lot of ground before getting to one huge topic that is often controversial when I present it.

Stop using retail therapy. I am saying this to myself as well. Most of us are guilty of it. We buy things not to satisfy a material need, but to fill some strange hole. The utility we feel declines quickly because we aren't satisfying the actual need we have for the product. Really look at your spending and narrow it down to fewer, but better items.

Be very careful about falling into the transactional utility trap. It is ok to buy a beverage and hot dog at a concert and pay $126 or whatever. Every now and then. It's not ok to go to Starbucks every morning to buy (crappy) coffee you could make at home. At some point paying for convenience will eat into your budget and damage your long-term finances. Pick your spots and go crazy. Don't bleed yourself dry.

Spread out your entertainment and fun purchases. You need to be mindful of the marginal impact on utility. Allow your financial taste buds to completely reset before you go back for more treats. By spreading the occasional splurges out over time, you will maximize their emotional impact and gain maximum utility. This will in turn allow you to spend less since you will be receiving the full benefit of the price you pay.

Have a conversation with your significant other about your money values. It is important for the other person to understand what you value (in money terms) so they can adjust. A budget will be very difficult to build if the two people are completely different pages.

Now for my final advice. This is specifically for married couples, young people considering getting married, or anyone else who might have finances mingled with another person. You should seriously consider an allowance for each other. I know this sounds absurd. Believe me, I do. I have heard every critique of this advice you can come up with. Yet, I know it works. So, I keep recommending it. Here is why a weekly spending allowance works. It removes the difference in utility completely.

Follow the process with me. My wife and I can sit down and agree on our budget. We can look at numbers on a page and remain completely emotionless about it. We have goals and we lay out a financial plan to reach them. This means moving those little numbers around. The numbers are not connected to any item or experience. They are just numbers on a page. We can then agree to a certain allowance for each of us that doesn't harm our budget or goals. It's just another number on the page. We are in full agreement as to the allowance amount. If we don't agree, we can discuss it COMPLETELY within the confines of the budget itself. No emotion. Once we agree, we can then set up our own small accounts where the allowance will go. From there the money is "gone" from our budget. It no longer matters at all what the money is spent on. The specifics make no difference. She buys what she likes without regard to my feelings. I do the same. At no point is there any reason for us to have a "utility" fight. This is one small step you can take that could go a long way to saving your marriage.

Chapter 30
Status Quo Bias

"I don't accept the status quo. I do accept Visa, MasterCard, or American Express." – Stephen Colbert

Brain Games:

When was the last time you shopped around for the following services?

- Insurance
- Bank accounts
- TV packages
- Cell Phone packages
- Mortgage rates or plans
- Any other financial services

My guess is of those listed you have recently looked into cell phones and maybe television packages. Why? Those expire. Your phone plan is on some version of the carrier's two-year plan. When it comes up, you are relentlessly hounded until you get a new phone and sign up for another two years. Same kind of deal with the television. Both cable providers and satellite providers seem to hate their current customers. The only way to get a decent deal is constantly switching. Yet, when was the last time you shopped for your insurance products? All of them. This is normal because we are lazy. We only have so much mental energy to go around. If something is currently working, why change it?

Tech Support:

Status-Quo bias in finance causes us to favor the current state of our financial affairs. We are resistant to changes or adjustments in our investment strategies or financial decisions. This leads us to maintain our existing allocation of assets and financial products, even if better alternatives or opportunities are available.

Key features of the status quo bias in finance include:

- Inertia in Investments: Investors influenced by the status quo bias don't bother to rebalance investment portfolios, even when market conditions or personal circumstances change.

- Preference for Familiarity: We stick with familiar financial products and services, such as keeping money in a bank account we have used for years, rather than exploring potentially higher-yielding options.

- Overemphasis on Past Decisions: We anchor on our past decisions, believing our previous choices were sound and continuing with them despite evolving market conditions.

Mad Money:

The status quo bias results in missed opportunities for improving our financial performance and achieving long-term goals. By sticking to the current state of affairs, you could overlook better investment strategies, higher-returning assets, or more cost-effective financial products. Let's go see what our friends might be doing wrong.

Jennifer has been using the same bank for her savings account since she was a teenager. This is where her parents have their bank accounts and Jennifer believes all banks are the same. Even though other banks offer higher interest rates and better terms, Jennifer feels comfortable with her current bank and is accustomed to its online banking interface. Despite the potential benefits of switching to a different bank, she remains loyal to her existing account out of familiarity and the desire to avoid change. Heck, she doesn't even bother asking if her own bank has better account options.

Our other buddy, David, has held the same investment portfolio for several years. He has only stocks in his accounts even though he has been warned about the risk of not diversifying. Now, David is turning 60 and eying retirement, but David still hasn't made any adjustments to his portfolio. He sticks with his current investments because he's used to them, even though a different allocation might better suit his current needs and risk tolerance. He is running the danger of a market downswing severely hampering his retirement outlook.

Jill has been using the same insurance provider for her auto and home insurance for many years. She hasn't reviewed her coverage in a while, and it turns out she is still paying for features she no longer needs. Jill purchased a second car for her weekend joyrides, but still has rental insurance on her policy. This makes no sense with an extra car now available. In addition, Jill had a pool installed and forgot to inform her insurance carrier. This leaves her open to huge liability losses if someone should get hurt in the pool. She simply maintains the status quo by renewing her policies each year without considering whether she could get better coverage or rates by exploring other options.

Travel Tips:

I joke about this being called the "Lazy" bias. However, the truth is the Status Quo bias is so powerful because we all have limited mental capacity and energy. If your current situation is not causing you massive pain at this moment, then it can be put off. At least, that's the thinking behind it. In order to overcome this bias, there must be an active plan. Try to follow these steps:

Establish a dedicated time slot on your calendar to review key financial decisions. This includes your insurances, investments, bank accounts, and other major items like a will or trust document. I would suggest at least once a year.

Actively shop the items that change price often. You may do your review and think to yourself, "my auto insurance rate seems reasonable". However, you likely have no idea what is happening in the market. Your assumption could be off by hundreds of dollars.

Finally, listen to your gut all the time. When you open your cable bill and your first reaction is, "man that seems high", its likely because it it. Somewhere along your daily journey you came across some piece of information and your brain captured it. It could have been nothing more than a commercial on TV while you were scrolling Tik Tok videos. You paid zero attention to it, but your brain caught something and stored it away. If your gut tells you something is off about your payments or accounts, listen to it. The brain is a funny machine.

Defeating this bias really comes down to understanding and accepting change. Most people think of finance as a static, boring topic. Yet, give some thought to how much has changed in the past ten years alone. Auto insurance companies have introduced driving trackers. Our phones now have apps to purchase fractional shares of stocks. Brick and Motor banks are being replaced by digital ones. Heck, you can apply for a mortgage, be approved, and sign the documents without ever seeing a real person. If you are still relying on services or products more than a couple years old, there is a good chance you are either overpaying or getting lack luster features.

Part 5: Overcoming Biases in Financial Planning

The final part of this book is designed to help you tie the impacts of behavioral biases directly to various parts of your financial life. I promised early on this book would be about changes you could make in your life, starting immediately. There is no sense in learning a bunch of technical jargon if you can't put it into practice and see a positive difference in your finances. While I could certainly go through this exercise for every part of personal finance, I am choosing to focus on the Big 3. The reason for this is simple. They affect every single person. These three are Budgeting, Investments, and Insurance. The simple truth is if you can't get these three pieces working correctly in your financial plan, the other pieces and parts won't matter. There will be no reason to worry about estate planning if you either don't invest enough or don't protect what you do have with insurance. There is no reason to focus on tax avoidance strategies if you don't even have a solid budget built. In the end, building a workable budget, investing in your future and protecting what you have are the core to any financial goals you might have. For this reason, I will target our conversation on those areas.

Chapter 31

Biases in Budgeting and Financial Planning

"A budget is more than a series of numbers on a page. It is an embodiment of our values." – Barack Obama

I want to begin this section by clarifying the title of chapter. In the field of personal finance, the term "Financial Planning" really means a whole range of topics. True financial planning includes budgets, insurance, estate planning, taxes, investments, social security planning, employee benefits, and more. For our purposes here I am referring specifically to budgeting and setting money goals. This is step one to building a financial future. You need to decide what your goals for money are over the course of your life and then give your money a job. However, far too many of us avoid even these basic steps to achieving financial independence. So, maybe we should look at why we refuse to help ourselves and what biases might be sabotaging our efforts to build a foundational budget.

From my perspective there are four huge psychological hurdles to budgeting holding us back:

- **Self-Control Bias**
- **Framing and Reference Point**
- **Mental Accounting**
- **Utility**

I am going to begin by wrestling the giant gorilla in the room. His name is Self-Control Bias. This giant ape is the main obstacle we face when we consider developing money goals and then building a budget. As we discussed earlier, the Self Control Bias in simple terms means we want what we want, and we want it now. We are not programmed to delay gratification. This leads us to ignore long term goal planning because that is the future and doesn't matter. We also don't build a budget because that might mean we don't get to buy exactly what we want today when we want it. I am hoping to convince you here and now that this thinking is exactly backwards. Budgets are not an anchor holding you back from buying what you want. No no no. A budget is the key that unlocks your chains.

People think of budgets as a tool used to control what you spend. That is only a partial truth. When used correctly, a budget is a road map to give your money directions. You get to decide where those directions lead. We all tend to think the budget guidelines are somehow coming from an outsider. In fairness, if you have never built a true budget before and your financial advisor is suggesting that you start then it's kind of coming from the outside. That's when our Self-Control gorilla starts to fight back. He doesn't like being told what to do. But what if you are the one deciding what to do? Your budget is the tool that makes that happen. By establishing YOUR priorities, you get to decide where YOUR money goes. If, like most people, you are in the vicious cycle of buying something you are not sure you can afford and then beating yourself up for it, it's time to take control. By developing a budget based on your desires and goals you can free up money to buy the things that matter to you. You specifically place those items in your budget. In doing so, you will strip the Self Control gorilla of his power.

The best example I can give is families who like to eat out. I have already made my opinion on this clear. It's a waste of money to me. However, that's my utility value of dining out. It might not be yours. You have two choices when it comes to eating out. You can ignore budgeting as an evil tool used to control you. By choosing this option, you get to feel anxiety and stress every time you eat out because you know deep down it's not a solid financial decision. This robs the moment of some of the joy. The other option is to embrace budgeting and specifically choose to include an amount for dining out every week in your plan. This results in a feeling of tremendous freedom to do something you enjoy with no second guessing. Your plan has given you permission to do exactly what your gorilla wanted.

The second little gremlin doing its best to get in the way of us building a solid budget is our Reference Point. I will put this in terms you can readily understand. Another name for this specific version of the bias is "keeping up with the Jones". It is incredibly hard to build your budget when you are constantly focused on what the neighbors have instead of what you want. When we allow our reference point to be someone else's position in life, it becomes almost impossible to achieve satisfaction. There are several issues that arise in our budgeting and money goals when our reference point is out of alignment with our reality.

The primary hurdle to overcome in our reference point is the ever-expanding horizon of where that reference point can originate from. Before the rise of social media, people compared themselves to their local neighbors. This was problematic in its own right, but at least it was localized. It is highly unlikely you live close to people in stratospheres above you on the socio-economic scale. That's not how neighborhoods work. In fact, some studies show a little amount of friendly competition can be good for you as you strive to be better. Now, however, people are comparing themselves to others from all over the globe. They are setting money goals and creating budgets (or not) that are not realistic or healthy for their situation. I live in a nice neighborhood and enjoy a comfortable upper middle-class life. In comparison to my local community, I am satisfied with my achievement. This means my budget can reflect reasonable expenses and I am quite happy from day to day. If, on the other hand, I were to spend all day on social media comparing my life to the make-believe versions crafted by "influencers" I would grow highly unsatisfied. I don't get to drive a Lamborghini and go to Europe every other week. Never mind that those people don't either. It's all a show. Yet too many of us try to make changes to our goals and budgets to achieve what we believe our peers are. Our reference point has become so skewed that we can't identify our own happiness anymore. Let me simplify this. If you make $500,000 a year, you should absolutely be living a great life and feel satisfied. Unless your reference point is Lebron James. Then you feel poor and dissatisfied. Make sure your reference point is your yesterday. Did you get better today. That's all that truly matters.

Next up on our journey through budgeting is Mental Accounting. Recall, this is a bias where we tend to break money sources up in our head and place them into different buckets. This ignores the reality that all revenue sources still end up in our bank account. We use a strange brain game to parcel our money out and treat different sources differently. The best example will always be the classic tax refund. Every year millions of Americans receive a tax return around February. Every year, Americans buy a whole bunch of TVs in February. Weird that. When I ask people why they bought the TV the response is normally some version of, "it was extra money and I have been wanting one for a while". Then I ask, "were you planning to buy a TV this year?" The answer is always no. So, they deviated from their initial budget and money goals for no other reason than the money seemed to come from a magical "other" source. That is Mental Accounting at its finest and we need to stop doing it.

The issue of Mental Accounting becomes so problematic because it causes us to splinter our focus and abandon a unified plan. You have one life. Financially speaking, you have one set of goals. Those goals are typically stated in the form of some type of outflow. For example, you could be aiming to invest for retirement, pay off debt, or save for a child's college expenses. These are all on the "backside" of the equation, meaning the money is exiting your bank account (at least temporarily). While you are most likely using various accounts to accomplish these goals, that is NOT the same thing as Mental Accounting. Paper accounting is the completely acceptable method of tracking various financial accounts to accomplish different goals. I support that. Mental Accounting is creating an artificial and invalid divide in our brains based on nothing more than the source of the money. Whether you have three or ten financial goals, all your income should be directed towards those goals. This gives your financial life cohesion and avoids the trap of unplanned spending. Using the tax return example, let's reframe the situation. When you are building your budget at the beginning of the year you should know if you are going to receive a tax refund. Add that estimated refund into your total income for the year and then plan accordingly. It is highly unlikely a TV was on your priority list. If, after you have covered all your planned expenses, there is money left over than fine. Go ahead and PLAN to buy the TV. This literally keeps it within your plan. However, stop pretending it is somehow bonus money you can just blow.

The final monster in budgeting biases is Utility. This can bubble up on anyone, but I am going to focus my points on readers with a financial partner. Whether it is a spouse or simply someone you share a budget with (say minor kids you are helping learn about money), the challenge of utility will come up. Utility is the idea that we all place different value propositions on items and experiences that have nothing to do with monetary value. This leads to massive conflict when people disagree about a value that can't be debated on a piece of paper. So where do couples go wrong?

The primary challenge I face when working with couples who are having money disagreements is getting them to understand it's not actually a money fight. They are rarely, if ever, fighting about the actual money. Instead, they are arguing over their value proposition of the item or experience. To redirect a couple, I might ask them specifically to place the argument back in the sphere of money alone. For example, if a wife is upset that her husband spends $50 every Saturday on golf, she believes she is mad about the $50. When I begin asking questions though, it is rarely the $50. It is more accurately described as her not thinking golf is worth it. She doesn't care about the sport. She doesn't understand why he wastes money on it. She could never get $50 worth of enjoyment from it. This can be proven with a couple questions. First, I ask, "what if the golf was only $15?" Most of the time her response doesn't change. She still thinks it's stupid. Then I ask her, "What if your husband decided to direct the $50 towards *fill in the blank* family goal (pay off debt, pay down mortgage, Christmas fund etc.)? Normally this changes her response. Now she is on board. What didn't change in this scenario? The $50. It was never about money. It was always about the utility of golf for HER.

This difficulty of budgeting increases when two people have widely differing utility for various items in the budget. Those items will always be the point of contention, even if they represent a minor amount in the overall budget. This is where those fights begin to take place. No one argues about the mortgage, car payments, groceries etc. Most people have a similar utility for these items. You know, they like to eat and sleep under a roof. The discretionary line items are where the fights happen. Yet, in percentages those items are small fraction of your budget. Couples with $4,000 worth of fixed expenses (housing, vehicles etc.) end up fighting over $50 worth of golf. To solve, or perhaps sidestep, this issue I always recommend couples give themselves an allowance. Together the couple agrees on an amount that is moved offsite (different bank account, cash, whatever) for each of them. Once the money is moved, they are each permitted to do anything they want with it. This short circuits the utility conflict because they agreed on a dollar amount. There is no way to argue about the "value" of a dollar amount. This means emotions are removed entirely. If the wife is ok with $50 coming from the budget, then the conversation is over. This is what I mean when I say move the conversation entirely back into the money realm.

Chapter 32
Influence of Biases on Investment Strategies

When it comes to the topic of behavioral biases impacting personal finance, the most common subject is investments. There are multiple books written dealing only with this topic. In fact, this is one of the reasons I chose to develop this book. I thought the industry was ignoring most of the personal finance topics in favor of this one specific one. All of that said, I do understand the importance and impact of the biases on your investment plan. I believe the reason for this is simple. Most people don't truly understand their investments or their investment plan. Many people vaguely understand the importance of investing for the future, but that is about as far as they can take it. So, the void of information and awareness this creates is quickly filled by shortcuts in our brain. After all, that is what heuristics and biases do. They give our brain a shortcut to fill in gaps quickly. As we have seen over the past how many ever chapters, this can be dangerous in many cases. So, let's summarize the biases that directly impact your ability to build and sustain a successful investing strategy for the long term. While I could likely re-list every bias from this book (and more) I want to stick with the five I believe have the most significant and potentially damaging effects.

Top 5 Dirty Investment Biases
- **Loss Aversion**
- **Overconfidence Bias**
- **Status Quo Bias**
- **Availability Bias**
- **Herd Mentality**

I am going to start this reflection with the bias I believe has the most damaging impact on our investment planning. Herd Mentality. I would not go so far as saying this is the most common bias on investments. I just believe it is the most potentially impactful.

Throughout the chapters of this book, I showed examples of herd behavior happening in real time and crushing the dreams of people. The GameStop saga was a glaring example of this that has happened very recently. As people rushed to join the frenzy, they failed completely to evaluate the actual investment they were signing up for. Any financial expert with even novice stock analysis experience could have warned people against GameStop stock. It was a loser for a reason. The financial fundamentals were simply not good, and the long-term prospects of the company are dim. Yet, none of that mattered. Once the public got wind of the feeding frenzy through social media, the whirlwind was inevitable. In the end, investors who could least afford to take losses took the largest hits. It was a surefire winner, until it wasn't.

I think what makes Herd Mentality so dangerous in the world of investing is who leads the charges. Many of our "gold rushes" are led by social media influencers and talking heads on TV. Neither of these groups have any clue about anything. They are ignorant of the topics they spout on about. This means you have the blind leading the blind. The other reason Herd Mentality is so damaging to our investments is because it involves OUR MONEY. If you get suckered into a fashion trend (like stupid Crocs, or sandals with socks) and end up looking like a fool, it's just pictures you must live down. If you follow the herd over an investment cliff, you are robbing yourself of a future. So, take caution and take a deep breath before you invest. If everyone else is jumping on the bandwagon, then whatever "hidden" value was available in the investment is already gone anyways.

The next bias I am always concerned about for investors is the Availability Bias. Unlike Herd Mentality, which only strikes occasionally, this bias is always in play. We simply have no way of avoiding the initial impacts. Our brains are hard wired to answer any challenge or question with the information it already possesses. That, by definition, can only be the information we have immediately available to us. As we saw in the chapter dedicated to this bias, however, that is dangerous. Our localized view is often incomplete or flat out wrong.

The availability bias affects whether we invest at all (based on friends and family experience), what assets we own, how much we think we need to save, and more. We take in the information around us and form a picture of what investing looks like. That picture is often distorted though. Here are some of the specific things to look out for as you build your investment plan and try to avoid this bias.

You need to make sure you have a diversified portfolio consisting of many different asset classes. Our tendency is to own only Large Cap stocks (Apple, Tesla etc.) because that's all we hear about, and all our friends talk about. In truth you need to at least consider Mid Cap stocks, Small Cap stocks, real estate, high yield bonds, government bonds, municipal bonds, commodities, derivatives and more. If you don't currently know what any of those things are, then you just proved my point for me. I am not saying you need them all. You just need to be AWARE of them all so you can make an informed decision.

The next thing you need to do is consult with an expert. This doesn't mean paying an advisor in every situation, but you need to talk with someone who knows what they are doing. The issue with Availability bias is you don't know what you don't know. Allowing someone else to assist you will automatically introduce new information to the equation.

The final advice for reducing this bias is to stop considering your immediate circle of people as representing the entirety of investors. If your parent had a bad experience with a 401(k), that means ONE person had a bad experience. If a buddy got lucky and had a stock surge 30% in a month, it doesn't make him an expert on stocks. He got lucky. Expand your horizon to encompass as much reliable and accurate information as possible.

The third bias impacting our investment plan is Status Quo bias. This is what we jokingly called the "Lazy" bias. That is a tongue and cheek description because the reality is most people simply choose to use their limited mental energy on other things. When it comes to our investment planning though, we need to commit some brain power.

The main reason this bias can be potentially damaging to our financial future is because our circumstances constantly change. The best investment plans are designed around the factors of your life as we know them best in the present as the plan is developed. This means the plan has limitations, by definition. It is your best attempt at evaluating where you are headed in the future and allocating resources to the right investment choices to meet those goals. Financial plans are heavily influenced by things like your time horizon, risk tolerance, income levels, family situation etc. If any of these change, then you need to review and revise the plan. By allowing Status Quo to kick in, you are potentially operating under a financial plan built for a different person. The person you were many moons ago when the plan first started. I have seen people wait too long to adjust their asset allocations for example. They stayed 100% invested in growth stocks well into their late 50's, when they had less than a decade to retirement. Then the market took a dive, and it was too late to recover. Stay on top of your plan. Simply sticking to what has always worked ignores the truth that you are not the same person you were when the plan was written.

Number four on our list of problematic biases for investing is Overconfidence. This bias leads us to believe we are better at this whole investing thing than we really are. The truth will always be that the market knows best. Very few (tiny fraction) people can outperform the market. The downside risk to attempting it is so severe that I would have a hard time justifying it. There is a reason that simple straight forward indexes outperform over 85% of actively managed funds. The active funds are being managed by some of the most intelligent, highly trained, and experienced financial professionals in the world. Yet less than 15% can claim to beat the market. Do you believe you are going to beat the market consistently?

Overconfidence also leads us astray by convincing us to ignore risk levels. It doesn't matter if you are investing in stocks or starting your own company, there will be risks you simply can't control. The best stock picker in the world will lose money if the market begins to drop. Boats rise and fall with the tide. If you start a business and invest your life savings, you are counting on yourself to be the driver of success. This confidence may be important to stay the course during tough times. However, overconfidence can lead you to falsely believe you can overcome any challenges. After all, you are amazing. Just ask yourself. What happens though if a recession hits at exactly the wrong time. It won't matter what your skill level is if the economy gets hit with a hammer. Acknowledging the risks and taking precautionary steps well in advance can keep your ego in check and prevent you from getting over your skis.

The final bias wreaking havoc on our investments is Loss Aversion. This is the king daddy of the bias in any book you read on the impact of behavior on investment planning. As humans we are preconditioned to hate losses of any kind. If we can't recognize and overcome this bias, we will become paralyzed and unable to invest sufficiently. The truth of investing will always be there is a price to pay. I mentioned in the chapter on Loss Aversion that the price of investing in anything is RISK. It is a baked-in part of the game. There is no world that exists in which you get to reap the rewards without accepting the potential for loss.

The key to overcoming this bias is to become good at converting risk into a price. For everything you purchase in your life, you know the cost in advance. This allows you to make a value judgment. Do you believe the price being asked is worth the product being offered. You are informed at the beginning of this process, and it allows you to feel more comfortable. For example, you instinctively know a meal you order at a restaurant might end up being crappy. You consider the price of the meal against the risk of a bad meal and make your decision. Try to imagine the same process when you invest. If I told you right now the cost of a comfortable retirement spent traveling and hanging out with your grandchildren was suffering through let's say seven out of forty bad years of the stock market, would you take that deal? When we frame the risks as a direct cost our brains are able to treat it the same way as a purchase. It certainly won't remove the fear of future loss, but it can place it in the right context and allow us to overcome it.

Chapter 33

Impact of Biases on Insurance Planning

"You don't buy life insurance because you are going to die, but because those you love are going to live." - Unknown

When it comes to insurance, we tend to view the topic as a necessary evil. No one really enjoys dealing with their various insurance products. Seriously, when was the last time you got excited about a discussion on your homeowner's insurance? Still, most people recognize this is a critical aspect of any strong financial plan. Without adequate coverage you are setting yourself up for a catastrophe. With this in mind, we can talk through some of the biases that are affecting your insurance planning and what you can do to overcome them.

The Biases preventing you from creating a solid Insurance program for your family:

- **Status Quo Bias**
- **Loss Aversion**
- **Endowment Effect**
- **Recency Bias**

We will begin our exploration of the impact of these four biases with the most damaging one for most families. Status Quo Bias. I mentioned the concern around insurance in the chapter specifically on the Status Quo bias. As discussed, most people simply don't like to think about insurance. It appears to be a "waste" of money to most people. While we all accept it serves an important purpose, we still view it as money spent on nothing. Honestly, it's one of the only products on Earth where you spend money hoping you never use the product at all. While that remains the best-case scenario, it also paints insurance in a wasteful light. In response to this, we tend to simply ignore it most of the time. After all, it's not directly benefiting us at the moment.

The Status Quo bias leads us into far too much complacency with our insurance packages. We go through the painful experience of setting them up once and then prefer to never see them again. As the circumstances of our life change, we never get around to updating the insurance programs. Even when we are forced to make a change, such as a new car purchase, we do only the minimum required. We call our agent and make the specific vehicle change. Did we review all the coverages while we were at it? Of course not. Whatever has been working seems good enough. This is dangerous though because the insurance hasn't technically had to "work" if you haven't made a claim. If you are currently paying for an insurance policy that is either missing pieces or lacks proper coverage levels, you simply got lucky. The insurance coverage hasn't "been working fine". It hasn't had to work at all. We purchase insurance for the future, however. Would that coverage still "work" if you must call on it next week?

I see the Status Quo bias hit all aspects of our insurance plan. Parents get promoted at work and receive the accompanying pay raise. Yet, they never bother to review or increase their life insurance. People get divorced and forget to change beneficiaries. Families buy an additional car for pleasure driving and then don't remove rental coverage from their auto policy. A person sells a used car and purchases a brand-new vehicle with a loan. However, they don't bother to remember adding the GAP insurance. Your family has a pool installed in the back yard but doesn't inform the homeowner's policy or increase the liability coverage. Your teenage sons turn 16 and start driving. You don't increase your liability coverage and/or purchase an umbrella package. (Excuse me for a moment. Both my sons just turned 16 and I need to make a quick phone call) Where was I? Oh yes, giving examples of simple everyday life changes that we fail to realize require insurance reviews. Honestly, it could be something as simple as price checking your auto insurance. Most people fail to price shop and once they get around to it, realize they are paying 15-20% more than they need to be. We have to be better at overcoming our desire to ignore our insurances and just assuming the policies are still working fine. I give more detail on this in the chapter on financial habits, but really this comes down to establishing both immediate triggers as well as scheduled reviews.

The second bias in play for insurance is Loss Aversion. The interesting part is this bias can play out both ways. We can purchase too much insurance or fail to purchase any at all. It depends on the lens we are looking through when it comes to avoiding loss.

The first detriment to your finances from Loss Aversion is purchasing too much insurance. It might sound strange to hear a finance person speak about having too much insurance, but I often find people paying for insurance they don't need. This can take on many forms, which we will get to in a minute. However it plays out, the issue always comes back to a crippling fear of loss. When we allow our brain to become consumed with the idea of losses, we tend to exaggerate the potential of those losses. We see the very worst outcome in every situation. This leads us to purchase insurance to protect against every possible outcome. The truth is most "bad" things don't ever actually happen. Even when they do, it's often far less severe than we fear. For every car accident resulting in destroyed cars and severe injuries, there are hundreds that result in only minor damage. This is even more pronounced in housing accidents. People tend to think of a home burning down to a total loss. That is extremely rare though. Most house fires consume one or two rooms and cause smoke damage. I am not claiming this is a positive outcome, but it is far from the disaster many people picture in their minds.

If we acknowledge people are suffering from loss aversion when purchasing insurance, what does it look like in practice? Most of the time this issue plays out as either coverage limits that are too high or completely unnecessary coverage. In both cases, we are paying more for insurance than is needed. Often, we would be better off lowering the coverages and placing the savings into an account for later. At some point you can become largely self-insured by simply stashing away the premium savings. Examples of this can be seen in most insurances.

When you purchase auto insurance you choose your deductible levels. Most carriers will allow you to choose increments from $250-$1000. The difference in premium between these two extremes can be as much as 10%. So, if your monthly premium is $100 per adult driver (roughly the Ohio average), you could be savings $20/mth based on a married couple. This means in just three years you have saved enough money to cover the $750 difference in deductibles if you stash it away. From that point forward all your premium savings go in your pocket.

Home insurance sees people overpaying for loss aversion in their Coverage C choices. This is the insurance coverage that pays for your personal property (think furniture, TV's, clothes etc.). Most insurance packages will automatically give you coverage on your stuff that is equal to 50% of the home's insured value. This means if your home is insured for $400,000, then your stuff is covered for $200,000. Can you see the issue here? You don't have anywhere near $200,000 worth of stuff. You are overpaying for insurance. You can ask your carrier to reduce the coverage and save some money on the premium. It might not be a much over the year, but every little bit helps. Especially when there is close to 0% chance you will ever utilize the full coverage amount.

My final comment on Loss Aversion in this context involves life insurance. For many people the worst fear they have is death. It is a subject they simply do not want to discuss. If we remember back, Loss Aversion is technically feeling the pain of loss more than enjoying equal gains. However, the aversion to this specific loss is so incredibly high that we never even consider it. We shut it out and pretend it can't happen. I am not trying to make light of this or poke fun. I have worked with many people who have such a hangup on talking about death that we can't discuss life insurance. Obviously, this can cause catastrophic financial loss for their family. I concede this version of Loss Aversion doesn't align perfectly with the textbook definition, but I believe it worth mentioning because of the potential for massive damage to loved ones if we don't address it.

The third bias impacting our insurance purchases is the Endowment Effect. Simply put, people insure items they don't need to. Most of us own items that are more valuable from an emotional standpoint than they could ever be from a monetary perspective. If you recall, the Endowment Effect states that we believe our possessions are worth more merely because we own them. We place higher value on our stuff than we would on the identical item if owned by someone else. This issue is compounded tenfold when it involves a sentimental item. We can find ourselves paying for insurance to cover an item that could either be replaced for relatively little money or we would not actually care to replace.

Let's look at a quick example to clarify what I mean. If you have a family heirloom sowing machine that has been passed down three generations, it likely means a great deal to you. You don't need to buy insurance on it though. If that machine was destroyed in a fire, there would be no need to replace it. You could purchase a newer machine that works better and any antique you could manage to find would have none of the family history attached. We should always keep in mind the primary purpose of insurance is to "make us whole" from a financial perspective. If you are buying insurance for any other reason, including to protect family history or emotions, then you are wasting your money.

The final bias affecting our insurance planning is Recency Bias. This bias creates an artificial view of the world based on the most recent events to happen. If your wife was in a car accident and totaled your Tesla just a few short months ago, you will view auto insurance very differently. If your home took storm damage and needed a new roof, but that event was fifteen years ago, you are going to push it to the side. Recency bias leads us to over inflate anything which happened in the near past. The closer to the event we are, the more impactful it is on our thinking. In some ways this makes perfect logical sense. If your spouse of twenty years had never been violent until the past three months, but is now hitting you every other day, you would rightly leave immediately (as you should). You would not need to weigh the previous twenty years into the equation. However, that is not how insurance works. Let's explore.

Insurance is based entirely on statistical models. The insurance carriers are making predictions about what might happen in the future. When they are given a large enough pool of people the predictions get scary accurate. This matters to you because it means any loss you have suffered recently is only one data point. The same goes for losses further back. The storm that damaged your roof may have been in the distant past, but that means nothing moving forward. You live in a certain area, with certain weather, in a certain kind of home. The insurance carriers can predict what the odds of you taking a roof damage loss are over the next year. That is how they price your homeowner's policy. The same is true with your auto accident. Just because it happened only three months ago, doesn't mean you turned into a bad driver and now it's going to happen every year. From this day forward you are part of the huge pool of people again, and you are priced accordingly. This is why many auto carriers offer accident forgiveness. The pure statistical odds say so many people will get into an accident every year. However, if it happens more than once you become an outlier, and your price begins to rise because you are no longer in the pool of people who rarely if ever get in accidents.

The important concept to take away from this section on Recency Bias is this. You must learn to distinguish between a recently occurring random accident, and a new developing pattern. If the loss was merely an accident, you have no reason to change your insurance program or overreact. If you sense a new pattern forming that does not appear random and it has a reasonable chance to negatively affect your future (crime has increased in your neighborhood with thefts), then you should take proactive steps to review your insurance program and ensure you are properly protected.

Chapter 34
Financial Habits

"Compound interest is the eighth wonder of the world. He who understands it, earns it. He who doesn't, pays it." – Albert Einstein

This chapter of advice is all about providing suggestions for financial habits that can help you fight back against the behavioral biases wrecking your financial future. There are active steps you can take to counteract the negative impacts of biases on your plan. As I have stated many times throughout this book, it is important to recognize the biases are happening. It is more important to be able to do something about it. So, this chapter will walk through a few different topics as we explore ways to provide yourself with insulation against the worst effects of the biases. Some of these suggestions have been touched on in various chapters, but I wanted to provide one concise location you can use as a point of reference for your action planning.

Processes Are What Matter.

My first piece of advice is to create processes for every piece of your financial life. I cannot stress this advice enough. Every component of your financial picture can be turned into a systematic process. By doing this, it allows your brain to evaluate the situation and decisions systematically. This will in turn immediately counteract many of the biases before they can even begin. Let me explain what I mean here.

When I teach my students about processes, I always use the car buying experience. I emphasize to them the importance of recognizing there is no difference in the car buying experience between them as young college students and myself as an older professor. We both must decide on the style of car, color, features we require, gas mileage we want etc. The PROCESS of evaluating and choosing a car is the exact same. The only difference is they have a budget of $5,000 and I have a budget of $50,000. Those are just numbers on a page. I keep saying over and over in this book that finance is NOT about math. It is about psychology. That holds true here. Regardless of your budget amount for a new car, you can build a process that will systematically walk you through a solid purchasing decision.

By developing processes, you wipe out or reduce several of the most concerning biases. Self-control bias is not an issue if you are walking through a process that removes the emotional component and focuses on facts. Mental Accounting can't take hold when you stick to an established process for every single dollar that enters your household. Narrative Fallacy, Anchoring, Diderot Effect and more are all held at bay because the process doesn't even consider them as a factor. If you establish a process that dictates 20% of your income goes towards retirement and is evenly split into five different Index mutual funds, how are Optimism Bias, Herd Mentality, or Recency Bias supposed to sideswipe your plans? If you create a process where you review your insurance packages every July 1 and January 1, Status-Quo bias becomes a non-factor. While we may be hardwired to be somewhat irrational at times, we can use the rationale brain we do possess to create processes which will shield us from the worst effects.

Automate Your Life

 Playing directly off my comments on processes, my next piece of advice is to automate absolutely everything you can. With technology these days you can create an entire network around yourself that is humming along without the slightest help from you. We can direct our paychecks into different accounts at the bank, so we don't have to worry about moving money to savings. We can use our 401(k) to automatically pull money into our investment accounts. We can set up bill pay for every recurring expense. We can set up reminders on our phone to alert us every July 1 and January 1 that it's time to review our insurance. We can have our financial software send us updates on our budget progress to avoid overspending in certain categories. The ways we can use these tools to automate our processes are almost endless, and it keeps getting better. More and more tools are coming to the market, and we should use them all. There are two massive ways that automation gives you an advantage over your biases.

First, the process of automating everything allows you to make hard decisions ONE time. We discussed all the various biases that can lead to poor investment decisions. If you decide you will manually move money from your checking account into an IRA every week, you are forced to wrestle the bias gremlins week after week. Was there something on the news this week that scared you (recency and availability biases)? Did you get a hot stock tip from your buddy (availability)? Is there a run on Tesla stock this week (Herd)? What is you just found out the new video game you really want is coming out a week early (Self-Control bias)? You are forcing yourself to overcome all the biases seeking to derail your plans over and over and over again. Eventually you will make mistakes. Even if you are "good" 90% of the time, it means thousands of dollars you claimed were for retirement did not end up going there. If instead of this mess, you set up an automated deduction from your paycheck directly into your retirement accounts you short circuit all the biases. You can muster the mental fortitude ONE time to make the right decision and invest your 20%. After that, you literally don't have to think about it anymore. (Please remember to set a yearly reminder to review so Status Quo doesn't rear its ugly face)

The second reason automation is so important is because it creates a way to immediately activate your financial plan. When you sit down and create your overall financial plan including insurances, investments, budgeting, savings, taxes and more, it is the most cohesive the plan will ever be. In addition, you are the most engaged and committed you are ever going to be. If you take the opportunity to ride the momentum and immediately set up all the automated processes to activate your plan, you are locking in the plan at the peak of flavor. The simple truth is much of what you decide in your financial planning session will require you to make certain changes. The longer you wait to make those changes the more the Status Quo monster takes charge. Additionally, by setting up the automated processes you can see results that much faster. This will create a sense of success and become a positive momentum builder.

Live in the Margin

A good rule of thumb when it comes to finance is to allow for margin. Margin is the small room for error that everyone needs in their life. This concept applies across your entire life, but today we are placing it in the context of personal finance.

The first place to create margin is your budget. Seems obvious and it is. Your budget should not be so tight, you can't make a single mistake. Mistakes are inevitable. If you are in a position where every single mistake derails your plan, you will never stick to the plan. To create this margin, you need to have small wiggle room in three ways. Start by undershooting your income just a bit. Unless you are on a set salary that never changes, you should lower your projected income a tad. If it turns out you make more than you projected, well no one complains about more money. Next, go into the variable expenses (groceries, gas, clothing etc.) and increase them a bit. I don't mean a major upward change. We are talking about a 5-10% increase. If you believe your groceries will be $150 a week, maybe consider setting the budget at $165. This type of adjustment will both protect you from a "bad" week and provide space to purchase a little extra if something is on sale and you want to take advantage by stocking up. The final step in this budget process is to add a category for miscellaneous expenses. These are quite simply those things that pop up that you could not have predicted. Your hope for this line item is that it never gets used. The cold truth we know, however, is that things happen. You will find the mental struggle of money to be slightly easier when you know there is a buffer sitting and waiting to do its job.

The second place to create margin in your finances is your investments. This becomes extra important when you consider the time frame we are normally dealing with when discussing our investments. Most of the time we are measuring in decades. If we needed some margin in our budget, which is normally a weekly or monthly thing, then we absolutely need it in our forty-year plan. When you make small mistakes in your budget, you see them quickly and can make the adjustment. If you make a small mistake in your investment plan you might not see the impact for years. By then it could be too late. It is also crucial to have some wiggle room on investments because reality tells us our powers of prediction are going to get worse and worse the farther out we push. If we can't accurately predict our grocery bill over the next couple of months, why would we think we can accurately predict our required income during retirement forty years from now?

To account for the concerns about our accuracy in predicting investment outcomes, we need to make two adjustments and gain margin. The first step is to reduce the estimated rate of return on our investments. While it is true the U.S. stock market has a one-hundred-year average return hovering around 11%, you would be wise to reduce that number a bit for your own planning. If the only way your plan works is by hitting that 11% exactly, you might be setting yourself up for a rude awakening in the future. Try setting your return rates at say 9% and see if the plan still holds. The second adjustment to make is the amount of money you invest. If you believe the math works at 15% of your income, try raising it slightly to 17%. This second adjustment is so critical because it is the part of the equation you directly control. The market return is out of your hands. You will be making an educated prediction (read: guess) no matter how much research you do. The market will be the market. Your chosen savings percentage on the other hand is completely your decision. Use it to create the needed wiggle room in the final outcome.

The third piece of your finances that would benefit from a little margin is your insurance. This can be both your property insurance as well as your life insurance. Let's begin with the property side. The main target of our margin mission here is your home. When you purchase homeowner's insurance, it will benefit you to purchase a plan that comes with automatic extended coverage. What this means is if your home is insured at let's say $200,000 and you have a fire that destroys the entire thing, the insurance company will allow up to $240,000 (20% is a common extended percentage) to rebuild the home. This small and typically free policy perk creates instant margin in your financial life. It means you are protected against either the value of your home increasing or the cost of materials increasing. It prevents you from needing to go back and revise your policy every year for minor adjustments upward. Even if the Status Quo monster is lurking, you have created a buffer for yourself.

The other side of insurance to create margin for is your Life Insurance policy. The reason for margin here is twofold. First, you will normally be buying Term insurance in ten-year increments. This is the most common policy type. In practice this means you pick an amount meant to provide for your family that will not change for the next ten years. Life insurance is typically purchased with factors such as age, health conditions, number of children, income level, marital status and more taken into consideration. Now look back over your previous ten years. None of those have changed? If any factors have changed then you really should be considering a new plan. However, that is not how we normally see it play out. Most people only make those adjustments when the ten-year term is up, and they are in renewal. So, to create space for changes over the next ten years it's good to have margin in your initial decision. If you run the numbers and believe the appropriate coverage level for yourself is $1,000,000, try purchasing $1,200,000. The cost difference on term insurance will be minimal, but the impact could be massive to your family. Keep in mind our discussion from the investment section. The farther out you are attempting to predict, the more margin for error we need to bake into the cake. If you are buying twenty-year term insurance, you will need to build in even more margin. Take a moment and try to imagine your life twenty years from now. It's hard right? Now imagine trying to calculate numbers you honestly think will hold true over that period. I'm sure you can hear your gut telling you we need to give more margin.

Asking for Help

My final piece of direct advice is this. Ask for help. Money should not be a taboo topic in your life. If we believe money is nothing more than a tool, then we should treat it as such. If you  picked up a weird looking tool at Lowe's and had no idea how it worked, you would ask someone. You wouldn't just go home and start randomly swinging it at things. On the flip side, if you have a very specific project you are trying to complete in your home remodel there will be a very specific tool meant for the job. You would ask someone what that tool is. Treat your money the exact same way. I want to make sure I am crystal clear on the two types of assistance you should actively seek out.

The first help to seek is from the experts who know what all those tools on the shelf are and what you can build with them. The obvious answer here is a financial advisor. Experts who are paid for their knowledge are a fine way to gain the information you seek in any field. However, I am not suggesting you MUST hire an advisor. There are lots of people running around who are extremely knowledgeable about money, but don't do advising for a living. You don't require a professional carpenter to explain how to use a hammer. You need to begin talking with people who know all the tools available in the financial toolbox and what goals those tools work for. If your preferred method of obtaining that information is a professional money manager, awesome. There are many amazing financial advisors who would be happy to help you in crafting a better plan for your financial life. If you believe you can get the information you need from your parents, that's cool too, assuming they know what they are talking about. The key point I am making here is there is no shame in admitting you weren't born a money wizard. News flash, no one is. Learning about money and all the various products in the financial realm takes time but is something every single person can learn. We all start out as novices. The only way you will get better at this whole "money" thing is to ask those people who are already better than you. So set aside your ego and your nerves and just ask the questions.

The other help I am suggesting you seek is very different. This help is meant for those people who are struggling with any of the topics I covered in this book. If you are unable to overcome any of the biases, or your money story is too filled with broken pieces, or your marriage is on life support because of fights about money, there is help available. I want to be absolutely clear here. I am not qualified to be that help. Very few people are. What I am referring to in this space is a trained and licensed Financial Therapist. These amazing counselors can assist you in exploring and overcoming many of the emotional and psychological challenges you are facing around money.

They help couples whose utility definitions are so vastly different they can't seem to bridge the divide. These professionals train in both psychology and finance so they understand the overlap and the challenges that occur when these two fields collide.

My most ardent advice is to any reader considering marriage soon. As a society we view it as normal to seek a marriage counselor prior to marriage to discuss things like careers, children, and family dynamics. We MUST expand that exploration to include finances. If you are thinking of entering a marriage without a deep conversation around all the topics in this book related to how money works for you, you are walking a dangerous path since we know money is a huge driver for divorce. However, this therapy is not just for couples. It is extremely helpful for anyone who can't find mental balance in their financial life. As I have repeated multiple times, personal finance is not about math but psychology. If this type of help is something you believe you need, then please reach out to a professional therapist. It will change your life. You can begin that search at:

https://financialtherapyassociation.org.

Chapter 35

My Family Plan

This bonus chapter is simply my explanation of my own family financial plan. When I began this book, I wasn't sure if this chapter would be written or even matter. After all, why would anyone care about our specific plan when every family has their own goals and plans. However, as I wrote the book it began to occur to me just how "heavy" the material can feel. In our journey together we covered a lot of ground. I can understand where you the reader might be asking yourself, "How can I possibly incorporate all this into my life?" That is a fair question. To help overcome this I see value in providing the foundations of the plan I use for my own family. My hope here is you come away with an appreciation for how simplicity rules the day. So, here is a quick rundown of how my family approaches finances in our life.

Budgeting and Spending Plan

This is the most important financial tool for my family. When it comes to money, I don't believe in anything as strongly as I believe in a solid budget. Our family budget guides our money to do the job we assign it. Here are the basics of how I build out our budget.

- I build a budget (and cash plan) that projects out the next year at all times. I update this projection weekly, meaning I am constantly pushing out a year into the future. This helps me ensure no surprises are coming down the road we are unprepared for. The process of weekly updating takes me about 15 minutes.

- Every bill we pay is done through some version of automation. Either the vendor takes it directly like our mortgage, or our bank sends it directly like the utilities. In any case, I do very little of the actual money moving.

- 20% of every dollar of income goes into our investment accounts. This is fully automated as well. My wife and I both have a 401(k) at work so those are deducted from our paycheck. The 529 plan for our children's college and our IRAs are taken directly by the investment companies.

- Every week I move a little amount into our "reserve" account. This is a temporary savings account meant to build up for known coming expenses. Think birthdays, Christmas (this comes every year at the same time people., stop being caught off guard), anniversaries, oil changes, school clothes etc.

- We avoid the "utility" issues most married couples face with the allowance plan I mentioned a few times in this book.

- We run every purchase we possibly can through our credit card. This allows us to build up cash back credits. You would be stunned by the amount of cash back you can build up with your everyday purchases. True story here. We recently lost a beloved family dog. Ruben was simply the best dog ever. When we (I) decided to get a new puppy, we were able to pay for everything (puppy, cage, food, initial vet visit etc.) with our points. Anyways, I pay off the credit every week during my Friday update.

- You don't care about my specific categories, but just know I build in about 5% margin on the various line items.

- Lastly, my children were all given debit cards (a child protected version, there are lots of apps available) when they turned 12. It is important they learn about money early and there is no better way than to make them spend their own money on things.

Investments

When it comes to our family investments, I keep it very simple.

- As mentioned above, we use our 401(k) accounts and IRAs for our retirement savings. We use 529 plans for college savings. Nothing fancy.

- Our investments are almost entirely Index funds. I use equal weightings in small, medium, and large cap stock funds along with a small portion in a bond fund and real estate fund. That's it. Again, there is nothing fancy about our investments. I trust the market to do its job.

- I have a small amount of money in individual stocks as nothing more than my chance to tinker. It makes me feel like a "real" investor.

- I set up an account for each of my three children with a stock purchasing app so they can begin learning about investing. I deposit (through autopay) money each week into their account. They decide which stocks to buy or simply add to the available index fund. I HIGHLY recommend you do something like this. The primary reasons people fail to invest are either being intimidated by the market or feeling like they aren't an "investor" (Imposter Syndrome). By introducing children to the market early, both are eliminated.

- I review our investment accounts and make any adjustments July 1 and January 1.

Insurance

Let's keep this really simple.

- We buy homeowners, auto, health, life (on both my wife and I) and carry an umbrella policy. All policies are purchased with a bit of margin baked in.

- I review insurance once a year based on the renewal schedule.

- See that was easy.

Taxes

- I use TurboTax to file my taxes. It takes me about 15 minutes.

- I use money to pay my taxes.

- Done.

Estate Planning

This is growing in importance to my family as my wife and I age a bit. We also lost a family member recently and it drove home the importance of keeping any estate plan updated. So....

- Craft a strong Will and FILE IT WITH THE COURT

- Review all your assets to make sure the Titles are done correctly.

- Create an emergency folder (digitally) that includes all account numbers, contact information, forms, etc. for all your major financial accounts. This includes bank accounts, insurance, investments, etc.

Well, that's all folks. I told you this doesn't have to be super complex. While there is indeed a whole universe of financial products available, most people don't need them all. I firmly believe 99% of people can build a solid financial future with a well-controlled budget, proper insurance coverage, a solid estate plan, and investing 20% of their income. Along the way, help your kids to learn about it as well. Done.

Chapter 36
Final Thoughts and Encouragement

"Make your goal more than money. Make it about helping people and creating a better future." – Maxine Lagace

As we close our journey together, I want to express my excitement for you. If you read this book, it shows you are interested in a better financial future. The good news is it can absolutely happen for you. There is nothing magical about money. Every wealthy family in history started with nothing. At some point, one person decided to get smart about this tool we call money and from that moment their wealth took off. It could be you and your family someday.

Before we say goodbye, I make a few small requests of you:

- Use your money as a force for good. There is no reason to have money if you don't help those around you. No matter how much money you have, someone has less.

- As you grow in your financial knowledge, share it with others. We need more financially literate people in this country.

- Share this book with others. I don't care if you let them borrow it, give them your copy, or buy another copy. It's a part of my mission to help others. So, help me do that.

- When you see someone else struggling with their own CRAZY MONEY, just ask, "How can I help?"

My very last comments. Look around and smile more. This is a wonderful life you have been given. Enjoy it and help others do the same.

-Jason